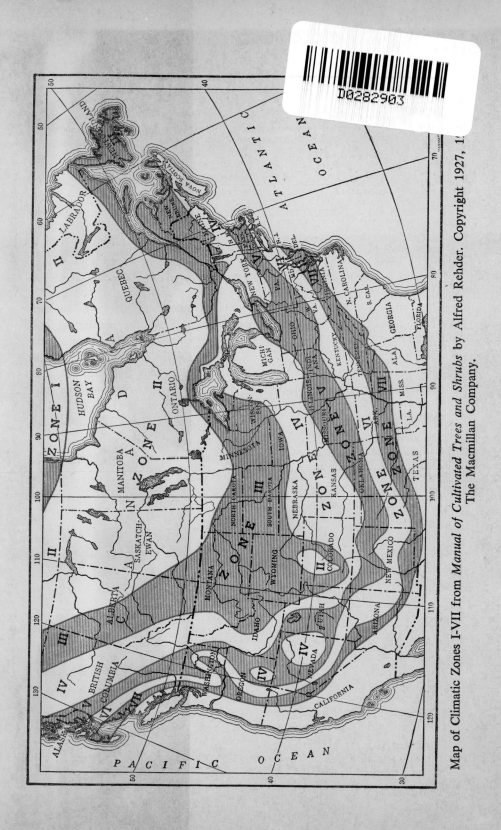

Map of Climatic Zones I-VII from *Manual of Cultivated Trees and Shrubs* by Alfred Rehder. Copyright 1927, 1[...] The Macmillan Company.

Evergreen and Flowering Shrubs
for Your Home

The planting need not be elaborate. The Lilacs in the picture are well placed to soften the end of the house. *Photographer, H. Armstrong Roberts.*

Evergreen and Flowering Shrubs for Your Home

by Katharine M-P. Cloud

New York

GREENBERG : PUBLISHER

Contents

PART I

HOW TO GROW SHRUBS SUCCESSFULLY

PART II

EVERGREENS FOR ALL-YEAR-ROUND EFFECT

PART III

FLOWERING SHRUBS FOR COLOR

PART IV

LIST OF SHRUBS FOR VARIOUS LOCATIONS AND USES

To my wonderful sisters
Beatrice and Dorothy
for their able and untiring
assistance

Foreword

Because she knows, loves, and has worked with plants over a period of years, Miss Katharine M-P. Cloud is admirably equipped to offer this book to home gardeners. She writes out of rich and fruitful experience, and as a landscape consultant she has learned the good points and the weaknesses of the evergreens and the flowering shrubs which she describes.

In this how-to-do-it age, the author, recognizing that home gardeners are more eager than ever to learn the art of propagation, has included a chapter on the subject. However, it is not in point for me to enumerate in detail the merits of this highly practical and useful garden book. Rather, it is my privilege and pleasure to commend it to the vast audience which I believe it will have.

Scores of garden books appear each year to fill the ever-growing demand for more information, new ideas, and practical suggestions. Some are more comprehensive and satisfying than others. But here is a book which fills a long-felt need, and hosts of gardeners will find it a helpful guide as they strive to improve their home grounds for greater livability and more outdoor pleasure.

Daniel J. Foley
Editor, *Horticulture* Magazine

Author's Note

In writing this book my thoughts have been especially with the small home owner. Being one myself, his problems are also mine. We all have the same objective, which is to gather around us all the beauty we can tuck into our gardens, however small or spacious they may be.

To broaden the usefulness of the book, I have included a few important tree forms of some of the shrubs. A selected list of evergreen ground covers is also given, since these plants play an important part in the gardens of today. Because roses are so universally loved and planted, a chapter has been devoted to their culture. Few realize, botanically speaking, that roses are actually deciduous shrubs.

The heights of the shrubs mentioned in this book must necessarily be approximate; these vary widely, depending upon soil, climate, and location. Ordinarily only a limited number attain their ultimate height in the average home garden. What to plant and where to plant are questions in everybody's mind, and the illustrations have been selected to give you planting ideas. The text will tell you how to plant, grow, and care for your shrubs.

My earnest hope is that in this book you will find the answer to success with your planting. May the keen pleasure and interest in gardening enrich your life. May your shrubs prosper and increase in beauty with the years.

K. M-P. C.

Acknowledgments

I wish to express my deep gratitude to Mr. Daniel J. Foley for the foreword which he so kindly wrote in spite of his many pressing duties.

My warm thanks go to the following who have given so generously of their time in reviewing certain chapters of my book: Dr. John L. Creech for reading the chapters on propagation and rhododendrons, Mr. F. Gleason Mattoon for reviewing the holly culture and Mr. Richard Thomson, rose expert and author, for his advice on several phases of the rose chapter.

Others to whom I would like to express my thanks for their expert assistance in various ways are Miss Gertrude Smith, assistant to Mr. John C. Wister, Director of the Arthur Hoyt Scott Horticultural Foundation of Swarthmore College, Dr. John M. Fogg, Jr., Director of the Morris Arboretum of the University of Pennsylvania and Dr. P. W. Zimmerman of the Boyce Thompson Institute for Plant Research, Yonkers, New York for information on Camellias. My gratitude also goes to Mr. J. d'Arcy Northwood, Curator, Audubon Shrine and Wildlife Sanctuary, Audubon, Pennsylvania.

I am also grateful to the Brooklyn Botanic Garden for their invaluable publications, as well as for those of The Pennsylvania State University and Cornell University. My thanks are also extended to The Pennsylvania Horticultural Society for their splendid co-operation.

I take this opportunity to thank Mrs. Walter W. Beachboard for her helpful editorial suggestions. My gratitude goes to Miss Carol H. Woodward and Mrs. William H. Leedy of The Macmillan Company for their kindness in arranging for the use of Dr. Rehder's zone map and zone numbers, which are an extremely useful addition to the book.

To Mary Alice and John P. Roche I send a special thank-you for their interest and generous contribution to the illustrations of the book. I am most grateful to Paul E. Genereux who has also added substantially to the illustrations.

Through the courtesy of *The American Home Magazine, Flower Grower,* the *Home Garden Magazine,* and *Horticulture Magazine* I have been given permission to use pictures from their magazines. My sincere thanks go to the editors of these publications.

Of the many books used for reference a few have been my constant companions. Because of the splendid help they have given me, I feel indebted to the authors of the following books: *Woman's Home Companion Garden Book,* John C. Wister;

Shrubs and Vines for American Gardens, Donald Wyman; *Manual of Cultivated Trees and Shrubs,* Alfred Rehder; *America's Garden Book,* Louise and James Bush-Brown; and the *Wise Garden Encyclopedia,* edited by E. L. D. Seymour. I wish to express many thanks to Dr. R. C. Allen for the assistance given me by his book *Roses for Every Garden.* Other books on roses that have been especially helpful are *Anyone Can Grow Roses* by Cynthia Westcott and *My Friend the Rose* by Francis E. Lester.

A word of gratitude goes to Mr. Elliott W. McDowell, Editor of Greenberg : Publisher for his helpful understanding along the way.

Katharine Mallet-Prevost Cloud

Ardmore, Pennsylvania

Part I

HOW TO GROW SHRUBS
SUCCESSFULLY

Chapter I

Shrubs Are Rewarding

Shrubs are fundamental. There are many gardens—"green gardens"—without flowers; but a garden without shrubbery lacks character and substance. Shrubs are the frame, the background, the foundation. They are, in a sense, a part of architecture. Without them houses rear up bleakly from the ground. An architect depends upon their lush irregularity to soften—or to stress—the straight lines with which he has to deal. Think of the houses you know, take away the *Rhododendrons,* the nestling *Azaleas,* the gleaming Hollies, the luxuriant Yews, and how harsh and naked they would look—how unwelcoming!

Through countless years, shrubs have played an important role in landscape design. In bygone days when places were large and pretentious, evergreen and flowering shrubs were used on a lavish scale. In today's gardens they assume a new importance because of the trend toward outdoor living and the need for seclusion from the neighbors. Pocket-size houses on restricted lots are the order of the day; the planting of shrubs can hardly be overestimated in designing these places.

The uses of shrubs are many. A walk or a driveway can be accentuated with a planting of bushes, either in groupings or as a hedge. In many instances an artistic grouping of shrubs on each side of the entrance to the property features an otherwise uninteresting approach to the house. A long stretch of wall offers a splendid opportunity for an attractive

13

This "before" picture shows the house at the time it was acquired. Heavy-growing evergreens smothered it and obscured the outlook.

A metamorphosis occurred when the old planting was replaced with appropriate shrubbery. The pink Flowering Dogwood is set off by the white blooms of *Azalea ledifolia*. An *Azalea Hinodegiri* to the right of the front door is well placed to give a vivid touch of color. *Owners, Mr. and Mrs. Loren F. Hildreth. Courtesy Flower Grower, The Home Garden Magazine. Photographer, the Roches.*

planting, and many a terrace can be set off with low-growing evergreen or deciduous plant material.

An outdoor living area that is well secluded from the neighbors adds greatly to the pleasure of family life; by all means include this in your planting scheme and you will never regret it. Plan it attractively so that it will be an extension of the house itself—a restful, comfortable haven for the hours of relaxation, as well as for easy entertaining—a spot set aside from the bustle of the outside world. For such a purpose shrubs are indispensable, whether it be an "outdoor living room," an intimate barbecue alcove, or a spot set aside for the children's playground. Because of the strong trend toward outdoor living, it has now become as necessary to decorate the grounds as it is to decorate the house itself. Shrubs also provide a satisfactory screen for any unsightly spots, such as the drying yard, trash cans, or the compost pile. The flower garden itself could not have a better enclosure than a background of shrubs, particularly the evergreen varieties.

Other uses of shrubs include the planting of hedges and living fences. Topiary work sounds pretty formidable, but as a matter of fact it is not difficult to accomplish, and this method of training plants provides an engrossing hobby. It is discussed in a later chapter.

Shrubs are permanent fixtures; they are rewarding, easy to maintain, and inexpensive; and those who do not want the exacting upkeep of perennials will find a shrub garden a real joy. These factors make them especially adaptable to present-day garden-making.

What a satisfying, lovely garden can be designed with a well-planned combination of shrubbery that follows the seasons! In order to carry on the color theme during the spring, summer, and fall months, select shrubs with different blooming seasons. One of the earliest plants to flower is the Chinese Witch-hazel, which unfolds its yellow blossoms in February in the latitude of Philadelphia, or even earlier if the weather is not too forbidding. Other harbingers of spring are the fragrant bush Honeysuckle and the decorative Star Magnolia. This bush form of Magnolia is profusely covered with star-shaped flowers which appear especially pure and dazzling in contrast to surroundings that have not quite dispelled the chill and dreariness of the long winter months.

Forsythia follows next, with its pale yellow bells borne gracefully along the branches. About the same time, Spirea Thunbergii adds its touch of white to the border, and in quick succession the lovely Bridalwreath Spirea is busily putting on its mantle of white blossoms.

This 15 x 25-foot terrace was turned into an enticing spot with *Azaleas* and a specimen Laurel. The pink flowering *Clematis montana rubens* forms a delicate tracery on the fence. *Owners, Mr. and Mrs. Loren F. Hildreth. Courtesy Flower Grower, The Home Garden Magazine. Photographer, the Roches.*

May dawns, and with it appear the decorative blooms of the Lilacs, so dear to the hearts of all flower lovers; the Lilac has been one of the most loved shrubs since days gone by. It is not definitely known just when this plant reached America, but probably it made its first appearance in 1737 when it was sent to John Bartram in Philadelphia. Washington, who was a frequent visitor at the Bartram gardens, probably obtained from them the Lilacs which he planted at Mount Vernon.

In May the glory of the flowering shrub season is at its height, so varied are the many plants which vie with each other in a gay display during that month. *Azaleas* commence to flower in April and continue into July; Deutzias, Flowering Almond, and Spirea Vanhouttei are a few of the many that literally cover themselves with blossoms. A little later on come

The terrace overlooks this colorful spring garden with its background of shrubbery. The border has been laid out in gracefully undulating lines. *Pachysandra* provides a carpet of green under the shade of the tree. *Owners, Mr. and Mrs. Loren F. Hildreth. Courtesy Flower Grower, The Home Garden Magazine. Photographer, the Roches.*

such favorites as Weigela, Mock-Orange, Beauty-bush, and Hybrid Rhododendrons.

In late June or July the Smoke-tree commences to open its feathery
panicles of dusty mauve which crown the tips of the branches and give
somewhat the effect of smoke. This is a distinctive plant which has been
grown in gardens for nearly two thousand years, and it is still popular
today. The Rose of Sharon, the Chaste-tree, and Hydrangeas all belong
to the group of shrubs that dominate the summer garden. In addition to
these, do not overlook the Butterfly-bush, so called because it is a mecca
for butterflies. The Arbutus-bush, which perhaps is better known by its
botanical name Abelia, in common with the Butterfly-bush, has the splendid characteristic of a long period of bloom—at least six weeks. As a
matter of fact, it is not at all unusual for the Arbutus-bush to flower from
late July well into October. Unless hard frost comes early the Abelia in
my garden still has a few brave flowers which withstand the light frosts
of early November.

In working out the planting scheme for a shrub garden, there are certain points to bear in mind. Select plants that have a good foliage effect.
The flowering shrubs should be limited to those that are showy either
when they are in flower or in berry; the brilliant colors of many of these
berries do much to brighten the fall landscape. The use of evergreens in
the planting rates high on two scores: first of all, for the contrast in color
and texture which they provide; secondly, for their luxuriant note of
green which adds a welcome note of interest to the dull winter months.

Chapter II

Shrubs Are Easy to Grow

We have all seen shrubbery plantings that are never watered, fertilized, or sprayed and yet live on year after year. These stalwart woody ornamentals will survive a remarkable amount of neglect; but in common with everything that grows, they respond favorably to good care. Proper maintenance, however, is not troublesome; it simply consists of some annual pruning, enough soil fertility to draw on for growth, and sufficient watering during dry spells. If these cultural points are observed, the planting will grow in stature and beauty with the years.

From the practical angle, one of the secrets of success is to select shrubs that will thrive in the existing climate, soil, and exposure. We cannot go against nature; but if we cooperate with her, she is a generous giver. As we all know, some plants are sun lovers, others do best in locations where they are partly shielded from the hot summer sun, while still others will flourish in the shade. A trip to your nurseryman will be of great value in determining your selection; he will help you decide which bushes will do best in your location and for your particular needs.

Soil Preparation. Any average garden soil will satisfy the needs of most shrubs, and planting can be done without previous preparation of the ground. However, better results can be had if the soil is given some preparation prior to planting. If the ground is fertile enough to grow vegetables, this preparation will consist of spreading a two- or three-inch

19

A foundation planting of evergreens blends this house into its surroundings. *Photographer, H. Armstrong Roberts.*

layer of well-decomposed cow manure over the planting area and turning it under to the depth of the spading fork; the soil is then raked to a level, well-pulverized tilth. If soil conditions are poor, it will then be advisable to remove the unproductive earth to the depth of a foot or so and to fill in the excavation with rich top-soil or compost, before adding the manure. Organic matter, such as manure, commercial humus, peat moss, compost, leaf mold, or green cover crops, adds humus to the soil. The value of humus and its reaction on the growth of plants is well described by F. H. King: "We should think of humus as the food of microscopic life in the soil, and of the waste products of this microscopic life as a very essential part of the food of higher plants. Keeping this in mind, we can better appreciate the importance of farmyard manure, for through its decay humus is formed. Both are organic matter partially decayed and capable of contributing food to higher plants." *

* *The Soil*, F. H. King. Courtesy of Mrs. F. H. King.

How to Plant Shrubs.   In planting shrubs, make the holes deep and wide enough so that the roots can spread out in their natural positions without being cramped or twisted. Make the planting holes deeper than the ball of roots in order to allow space to throw in some loose soil. This will help the roots take hold. The same theory applies to the width; this should be wider than the ball to allow ample space for packing freshly worked soil around the ball. Cut off all bruised or broken parts of the roots, using a sharp knife or pruning shears to make a clean cut. Deciduous shrubs are planted to the same depth that they stood before—deep planting all too often results in failure. However, this is not the case with evergreens, which will do better if they are set from half an inch to an inch deeper than they stood before. Work the soil firmly around and between the roots; then pack the earth by tramping or by using a tamper. Loose planting may cause the roots to dry out before they take hold in the soil. Be careful that no manure or fertilizer of any kind touches the roots. Fertilizers are discussed later in this chapter. When the hole is half filled with soil, water generously; and after the water has been absorbed, finish filling in the hole. A saucer of soil around the shrub will be very helpful in retaining an adequate amount of water. This saucer should be kept through the first season. In planting evergreens that require an acid soil, growth can be stimulated by tucking in some peat moss around the roots before filling in with soil. The amount to use will vary from a trowelful to one or more spadefuls, depending upon the size of the bush.

Naturally, transplanting is a shock to plants, because their food supply is withheld until the roots take hold of the soil and commence to grow. For this reason the most satisfactory time to move deciduous material is in the autumn after the leaves have fallen and the flow of sap is practically at a standstill. If the planting is done in the spring, try to get the bushes in the ground early, before the leaf buds unfold. In the vicinity of New York City, March is a good month for this work. When the planting is completed, cut the ends of the shoots back and keep the plants well watered for at least two weeks, or until the shrub is established and the new growth commences. Watering is particularly important in the spring when the warmth of the sun dries out the soil unbelievably fast. Over-watering of deciduous shrubs in the fall will tend to rot the roots. At that season the soil is damp and cold; and after the leaves have fallen, the shrubs are unable to throw off excessive moisture. In this respect evergreens again differ from deciduous plants in that they require copious watering before the ground closes. Their leaves remain

Shrubs used as an underplanting to trees give seclusion to this gay patio garden. *Photographer, J. Horace McFarland Company.*

green all winter long and are constantly giving off moisture; unless they are given an ample store of water before the winter sets in, they will dry out, and winter killing may result.

Nursery-grown stock becomes established sooner after having been transplanted than shrubs that have never been moved. In planting bushes that are balled and burlapped, it is much wiser to cut away all the burlap except the part that is under the shrub, in order not to break the ball of soil around the roots. This, however, should not be done until the plant has been set in the planting hole. Frequently nurserymen will send bare-rooted stock for spring planting. These plants have been kept in cold storage all winter long and they will grow much faster if they are given a thorough drenching before they are planted. If possible, soak them overnight, but if you have no container available for this purpose, heel them in and water thoroughly. To "heel in" simply means to open a trench deep enough to cover the roots with soil. The plants are placed close together in a row with the tops in a slanted position. This treatment will be a real help in overcoming the dried-out condition of the wood. When the planting is completed, a daily watering of the branches will soften the wood and facilitate leafing out.

Nurserymen are now experimenting with a plastic spray, Wilt-Pruf, applied just before transplanting. This spray coats the leaves and branches and thereby checks excessive transpiration for about one month. If this experiment continues to give good results, it will revolutionize the planting of woody ornamentals out of season and make it possible to move shrubs with safety during the height of the growing season. The purpose of this protective coating is to carry the plants through the most difficult period of readjustment after being moved. It does not prevent the gases from escaping from the leaves, nor does it hamper normal growth.

A leading nurseryman—Mr. Moore—has had great success with Wilt-Pruf; he has used it constantly for moving his deciduous material—both large and small specimens—in hot weather. Three hundred small Magnolias were successfully transplanted on the hottest day of summer. This test was especially valuable because the plants were close together in the rows; therefore they could not be lifted with adequate soil around the roots. Mr. Moore points out the absolute necessity of cleaning the sprayer and the nozzle immediately after use.

There is no rigid rule for the planting distances between the shrubs. The determining factors are the kind of bush, soil, and climatic conditions, and whether or not an immediate effect is desired. Generally speaking, the larger shrubs are spaced from five to six feet apart, whereas the smaller growers can be set two to three feet apart for mass effect.

Cultivation.   Deciduous shrubs planted in borders have the advantage over those set in sod because the soil can be kept well cultivated. The benefits of cultivation are many, for in addition to the neat, well-cared-for appearance it gives, it deepens and pulverizes the soil and increases its water-retaining capacity. Bacterial activities, such as decomposition and nitrification, are also greater in soil that is kept well worked. Consequently, because of the work of the bacteria, the store of plant food in the soil is turned into forms which can be utilized by the plant, and a vigorous, luxuriant growth results.

Fertilizers.   If the soil is rich and deep and the shrubs are growing satisfactorily, little or no fertilizer will be required. When soil conditions

A section of wall against the turf left unplanted avoids a crowded effect. *Architect, Harold G. Wilson, Photographer, Jacob Stelman.*

are poor, as is often the case close to houses, one or two applications of fertilizer will be decidely advantageous. These can be given in the spring two or three months apart, the first one applied in March. No nitrogenous fertilizer should be used after the first of July, because it stimulates soft growth that would be more liable to winter kill. A complete fertilizer such as a 5-10-5, a 10-20-10, or a 10-6-4 can be applied at the rate of one pound to one hundred square feet. This can be purchased at a garden-mart, seed or hardware store. The first number in the formula always represents the percentage of nitrogen; the second, phosphoric acid; and the third, potash. For example, a 5-10-5 fertilizer means 5 percent of nitrogen, 10 of phosphoric acid, and 5 of potash. It is broadcast around the shrub as far as its outer spread. A top-dressing of cow manure in either a decomposed or dehydrated form is a splendid fertilizer. The manure is worked lightly into the soil. Whichever fertilizer is used, care should be taken not to allow it to touch the branches or the roots. In using a commercial preparation sold under a trade name—such as Vigoro,

Espoma, Vertagreen, Holly-Tone, etc.—it is important to follow the manufacturer's directions as to the amount of fertilizer to apply, since the exact quantity varies with the different brands.

Plants that thrive in acid soils—such as Rhododendron, Laurel, Azalea, Andromeda, Leucothoe, and in fact all broad-leaved evergreens—should be supplied with sufficient acidity. This can be done by using Cottonseed Meal, Soybean Meal, or Sulphur, applied at the rate of one pound to one hundred square feet. Broad-leaved evergreens do best when they are mulched (a mulch is a loose covering over the ground to protect the plant roots) at least during the hot months. Most of these plants are shallow-rooted, and active cultivation of the soil is apt to disturb the surface-feeding roots. A mulch conserves soil moisture, keeps the roots cool, and adds acidity to the soil. Suitable materials for this purpose are peat moss, leaf mold made from the decay of hardwood trees such as Oaks, hardwood sawdust, and Pine or Hemlock needles.

Evergreens whose foliage has turned yellow can have their green color restored by using a foliage spray of chilated iron. To be fully effective, repeated sprayings have to be made as the new growth appears. To make the cure permanent, the soil should be analyzed to determine the underlying cause of the chloratic condition; it could be due to poor drainage or to a lack of soil acidity at nutrient level.

Pruning. Pruning shrubs is an important part of routine care; it increases their vigor by concentrating the flow of sap to a lesser number of branches. Unpruned stock is comparable to a stream which, spreading in all directions, becomes diffused and loses the force it might otherwise have if the flow of water were restricted to one main course. Under the guidance of the pruner, growth is directed in the proper channels, the natural grace and symmetry of the plant is preserved, all weak and useless wood is removed, and the sap is conserved to increase the strength of the remaining branches.

In pruning shrubbery, no general rule can be followed; each plant is an individual problem. Even the same kind of bush growing under the same conditions frequently requires a different treatment than its neighbor. This being the case, if a few of the fundamental principles are understood, the results will be more successful.

Nature herself is an ardent pruner, as is well illustrated by the dead wood found in the tangled growth of neglected shrubbery. It is not sur-

This *Forsythia* has been growing in the same spot for twenty-four years. It proves that an annual pruning keeps a shrub within bounds and maintains its vigor and youth. Throughout this period the old wood has been diligently removed. *Photographer, Caryl R. Firth.*

prising that dead wood should exist when we consider the life processes going on around us. Each branch is attempting to grow and compete with its neighboring bud and branch. The result is a continuing struggle for "the survival of the fittest." It naturally follows that more growth occurs than can be properly nourished by the root system and that only those branches that are especially healthy are able to withstand the struggle for life; hence the accumulation of dead wood.

With shrubs that are grown primarily for their bloom effect, the main objective is to keep up a supply of flower-bearing wood. The young wood is the most floriferous and the old wood should be kept removed; this will encourage the formation of new growth. Spring-flowering shrubs should only be pruned immediately after they have finished blooming, as they form their buds at that time for next season's bloom effect; therefore if these are pruned too late, a large proportion of the flowering effect for the following season will be sacrificed. The majority of shrubs belong to

Azaleas and evergreens have been combined to add a decorative note to this terrace garden. *Photographer, Paul E. Genereux.*

this class, such as Forsythia, Mock-Orange, Deutzia, Lilac, Kolkwitzia, Flowering Almond, Japanese Quince, and the early-blooming Spireas. Summer-flowering shrubs—such as Althaea, Hydrangea, Buddleia, Vitex, Abelia, and the late-blooming Spireas—flower on wood of the current season's growth; therefore the best pruning time for this class of shrubs is in early spring before growth commences.

In pruning deciduous shrubs, comparatively little trimming will be required, provided the work is done every year. This work will chiefly consist of shortening any over-vigorous shoots and removing dead and superfluous wood. Aim to keep the growth sufficiently well thinned to allow the shrubs to have plenty of light and a free circulation of air throughout. In this way all overly old and unproductive wood is discarded, and the development of young shoots is stimulated. To remove dead wood is important, because apart from being unsightly it provides a congenial medium in which decay and disease organisms flourish.

The shape of the bush must be given careful thought. Avoid pruning shrubs in formal, symmetrical lines as one would prune a Privet hedge. Their chief charm and beauty lie in the natural grace of outline characteristic of the individual shrub. The pruning should be done with a sharp knife or, better still, with regular hand-pruners. For removing the larger branches, long-handled shears or a narrow pruning saw will be useful. Avoid shaggy cuts—they invite trouble, and any large cuts should be protected with tree paint. As subsequent growth will take place in the direction in which the bud points, it is best in most cases to prune to an outside bud in order to keep the shoots from growing inward. Prune half an inch or so above the bud so the bud will not dry out before it commences to grow.

In the renovation of overgrown shrubbery that has not been pruned for years, the chief aim is to restore the former lines and productiveness of the shrub; drastically severe pruning is the only method by which this can be accomplished. The pruning can be done at almost any time of year, provided the bloom for the coming season is not considered. However, it should not be done at the end of the season, as the sappy, tender growth which is induced would not have time to ripen sufficiently to safely weather the rigors of a severe winter. In the locality of New York City, March is an excellent month for pruning shrubs for renovation purposes, and even if the spring bloom is sacrificed, the benefit of a full season's growth is gained, and this is a well-worthwhile consideration in the work of shrub renewal. Prune the shoots to be retained to within two or three feet from the ground and remove at the level of the ground all branches that crowd or cross each other, as well as those that are old or diseased. If a drastic renovation is in order, cut back the entire bush to about six inches from the ground.

It has already been mentioned that this severe pruning will produce a rapid new top growth. It is interesting to note that normally a perfect balance exists between a plant's root system and its top growth. The greater amount of crude materials absorbed by the roots, the greater must be the development of stem, leaf, and branch. Consequently, when a large portion of the top growth is removed and the root system remains intact, the same amount of crude material which has been utilized by the plant before the pruning will now be concentrated on a fewer number of branches. Obviously a large amount of vegetative growth then takes place, and the balance between root and top growth once more becomes normally established.

It is best to prune evergreens the first or second week in May, the purpose being merely to keep them compact and shapely, so that cutting back the branches here and there is all that is necessary, excepting the shearing needed when grown as hedges.

Espalier work is an attractive method of training shrubs. This simply means to guide their growth so that they will grow flat against a support such as a wall or trellis. By this method the plants are pruned to form a symmetrical design, with the branches trained into a vertical, diagonal, or horizontal pattern. The branches are fastened to the support at intervals. Young plants should be chosen for the purpose so that the needed cutting back of the shoots to form the desired pattern will be possible from the start. Any irrelevant shoots should be removed to keep the design clear cut. This practice is well adapted to small places where space is limited.

Winter Protection. There are various factors that enter into the question of winter injury, they can be summed up as follows: an inadequate supply of moisture before the ground closes (this is particularly applicable to evergreens); a lack of protection through the winter months for half-hardy shrubs and evergreens; breakage from snow; and burning from the bright sunshine after a snowfall in late winter or early spring when the sun is warmer. Another factor is beyond our control; if there has been an excessive amount of rainfall in the summer and fall, a tender growth may result that does not have time to mature before cold weather sets in, and is therefore more likely to winter kill.

Giving at least three heavy waterings to evergreens in the fall will do much to compensate for the loss of moisture through transpiration. It should be borne in mind that unlike deciduous shrubs, evergreens do not lose their leaves in winter; as a result, all year round they are throwing off moisture. When the ground is hard-frozen, the plants cannot draw from it the needed amount of water.

Some kind of protection in the cold climates for the first winter after planting deciduous shrubs, and for the first two winters after setting out evergreens, is of decided value. This may be only a matter of covering the ground around the shrub with salt hay, strawy manure, leaves, or evergreen boughs. In exposed locations, and always with half-hardy

A low, well-clipped hedge gives a finishing touch to the stone wall which holds the grade. *Courtesy Mahoney Construction Company. Photographer, Bill Harris.*

shrubs, a windbreak is advisable. This can be made of any durable material such as burlap, canvas, evergreen boughs, or straw mats that are on the market for this purpose. Stout stakes driven into the ground will support the screen, and heavy wire run from stake to stake will further fortify it. Box bushes are usually surrounded with burlap or canvas, and care should be taken to leave sufficient space immediately around the bush to allow a free circulation of air. The danger of breakage from the weight of the snow can be obviated by placing a covering over the top of the shrub; again be careful to allow space for ventilation. Sometimes wooden laths are used to break the fall of snow. If no protection is given, the snow should be brushed off evergreen bushes as promptly as possible; if it remains on the foliage, melting and freezing again, the sunshine will in all likelihood burn it. Cornstalks are sometimes used for a windbreak, but as they offer a home for rodents they are not very desirable.

The protection should be left on until all danger of a return of winter temperatures has passed. March is a tricky month; the high winds and increased warmth of the sun are as threatening to the welfare of the shrubs as is the winter cold. Often evergreens will come through the winter with flying colors, only to be harmed by the early spring days. When the ground is still frozen, the plants cannot obtain from it their needed amount of water, and as a result the foliage burns. A new way that is now being tried out to avoid this injury is to cover the plants with a plastic spray (Wilt-Pruf) in late winter to check the loss of moisture from the foliage. The spray is also being applied in early winter as a means of winter protection, thus doing away with the unsightly burlap and other materials which at present are generally used.

Insect Pests and Diseases. Control of insect pests and diseases has been immensely simplified since the introduction of all-purpose sprays and dusts. These preparations contain insecticides and fungicides that successfully combat a great majority of the troubles that plants are heir to. Most of the chemicals are highly poisonous and should be kept well out of the reach of children and pets. The manufacturer's directions must be strictly adhered to—too strong a solution will only lead to trouble. Whether a spray or a dust is used, complete plant coverage is a "must." The undersides of the leaves should be given the same protection as the upper surfaces. For the home gardener, dusting is far less troublesome than spraying; there is no measuring or mixing or cleaning out of the sprayer after use. The dust gun is easy and light to operate and can be kept filled for quick use. If a sprayer is used, any left over solution should be thrown out, because the evaporation of the water from the mixture leaves too strong a solution for future use.

One of the best all-purpose mixtures on the market is one that contains DDT, Malathion, Captan, and Sulphur. This preparation can be used either as a dust or as a spray; it is efficacious in combatting many insect pests and diseases. In fact, there are innumerable brands of pest controls available to the gardener of today. Whichever one you select, check up on the ingredients; if Sulphur is included, it will burn the foliage if applied when the temperature is in the nineties. And never use Sulphur on Viburnum bushes; Viburnum Carlesii is especially allergic to this fungicide. A good hot-weather substitute is Ferbam. If this chemical is mixed with Malathion, it will be effective against many insects as well as diseases. DDT and Malathion will stop the ravages of leaf-eating caterpillars and beetles that threaten to mar the luxuriance of the foliage and sap the vitality of the shrub. For combatting the weevils that feed on the leaves of Rhododendrons, Laurels, and other garden favorites, dust the entire shrub and the soil around it with Chlordane; water the soil where the Chlordane has been applied.

Bag worms are checked with Malathion applied in late June, before the bags become too large. Borers can be prevented by spraying with DDT. To be fully efficacious, three successive treatments at intervals of two weeks will be needed. The time of application differs with the kind of borer to be combatted. For example, in the case of Dogwood, spraying should commence the third week in May, whereas with Lilacs the correct timing is mid-April. For information other than that given under individual cultures, write to the State or Federal Department of Entomology, or your County Agricultural Agent. In fact if any problem arises that cannot be solved, one of these departments will always be ready to give you advice.

Scale on Lilacs, Euonymus, and other shrubs is eliminated with a dormant spray of Lime-sulphur or oil. This spray is only used once in a season. Lime-sulphur is unpleasant to handle, and it discolors brick, stone, and paint. Oil is much easier to use and is very efficacious. This is applied in early spring before the buds open; it should be done in the early morning when the temperature is between 40 and 65 degrees. Otherwise the oil may separate and cause the shrubs to burn. Whichever spray is used, it is most important to follow the manufacturer's directions carefully. During the growing season the gardener who has only a few bushes infested with scale can use Lemon Oil diluted according to directions; it can be applied with a small brush, which will rub off the scale.

Rotenone has the advantage of being non-poisonous to man and to pets, which is a strong point in its favor. It is useful for routing out sucking insects, and it is also effective in controlling some leaf-eating pests. Mixed with Dusting Sulphur, it provides one of the few non-toxic combinations, and this mixture can be purchased already prepared. The addition of Sulphur gives it value as a fungicide as well as an insecticide.

The tall Privet hedge provides an excellent screen for the outdoor living area, and sets off the colors of the many flowers in the border. Two American Hollies dominate the far end of this charming garden which is only nineteen feet wide. *Owners, Mr. and Mrs. Charles L. Matthews. Courtesy Flower Grower, The Home Garden Magazine. Photographer, the Roches.*

Chapter III

Hedges and Living Fences

It will pay off with satisfaction through the years to give the soil a thorough preparation prior to planting a hedge. Deeply worked ground with plenty of available fertility will stimulate growth and give the shrubs the right start in life.

There are two ways to accomplish this. One of these is to spread a two- or three-inch layer of well-rotted cow manure over the planting area and to fork it into the ground to the depth of the spading fork. The earth is then leveled and raked to a fine tilth. The second method is to ameliorate the soil to a depth of at least eighteen inches, by two feet in width. Any poor soil should be discarded and replaced with either topsoil or compost. In both instances well-rotted cow manure is worked into the ground. If it is not practicable to fill the entire area with rich soil, at least fill the planting holes with the best soil obtainable.

Before planting commences, open a trench the entire length of the line to be planted. This trench should be sufficiently deep and wide for the roots of the plants to spread in their natural positions. The soil is then filled in over the roots and rammed firmly around and between them. A garden line stretched the length of the trench will enable you to set the plants straight in the row. The exact distance between the plants will vary according to size, bushiness, and habit of growth. Generally speaking, plants a foot or less high are spaced four inches apart, while the

35

larger ones are set so that the outer spreads of the adjoining plants touch each other.

In the routine care of a hedge, pruning is of primary importance to maintain a compact, symmetrical growth. There are various methods of training a hedge: namely the rectangular, triangular, and Gothic arch types. The rectangular is more universally used than the other methods, and the upkeep is the easiest of all to maintain. However, in regions where the snowfall is heavy, this kind of pruning often causes severe damage from breakage during winter storms. A safeguard against loss of this kind is to prune the hedge in the form of a triangle. This is done by shearing the hedge to slope upward from the base to a point at the top. This way of training enables the sun to reach all parts of the hedge and lessens the danger of the plants becoming straggly at their base. This can also be said of the Gothic arch type. This kind of training is essentially the same as for the triangular method, the only difference being that the top, instead of terminating in a point, is rounded.

California Privet (*Ligustrum ovalifolium*), Zone (V), is widely used for hedge purposes, and a great deal can be said in its favor. It is rapid-growing, inexpensive, and easy to grow. It is excellent for seashore gardens because it thrives in salt air. In the North, California Privet is apt to die back during severe winters. This drawback, however, is not too serious, for the plants make a quick come-back during the growing season. *Ligustrum amurense,* the Amur River Privet, is very hardy and gives practically the same effect as the California variety. *Ligustrum Regelianum* (Regel Privet) is a very hardy, easy-to-grow variety, and its blue-black berries persist until the new leaves unfold in spring. South of Washington, D. C., *Ligustrum lucidum* (Glossy Privet) and *Ligustrum japonicum,* will thrive. Both are extremely handsome and satisfactory hedge plants. They have the asset of growing in the shade as well as in the sun.

For hedges five feet or less in height, Japanese Barberry (*Berberis Thunbergii*) is one of the most popular plants, and it thrives in most parts of the United States. In common with Privet, Barberry will do well by the sea. If a formal enclosure is called for, pruning will be necessary, but a Barberry hedge which is allowed to develop its natural form is much more graceful. Provided it is not pruned severely, the profusion of its scarlet berries, combined with the red autumnal tints of its foliage, will

The well-trimmed Arborvitae hedge makes this outdoor living room intimate and cozy. The Magnolia on the terrace and the nearby Flowering Dogwood give important variation in height and form. *Photographer, J. Horace McFarland Company.*

enliven the fall landscape. *Berberis vulgaris* will grow about two feet higher than *Berberis Thunbergii,* but it cannot be depended upon to make such a compact growth. For the North and Northwest parts of the country, *Berberis mentorensis* is a highly desirable variety. It forms an upright, compact hedge which requires relatively little pruning. *Chaenomeles japonica* (Japanese Quince) fits in splendidly in informal surroundings. The spring display of bloom is always decorative. It should only be pruned right after bloom. During the summer, straggly shoots can be cut back. Any drastic pruning done after the spring trimming will lessen or sacrifice next spring's bloom.

There are many beautiful evergreens which are well suited to hedge planting. *Thuja occidentalis* (American Arbor-vitae) is extremely popular, and it adapts itself to the varied climatic conditions of this country, however, in the colder sections it becomes discolored in winter. In the South, and in sheltered locations as far north as Massachusetts, *Thuja orientalis* (Oriental Arbor-vitae) can be used, and it holds its green color through the winter. *Buxus sempervirens* (Common Box) does well as far north as central New York state, and it is one of the loveliest of all hedges. *Buxus suffruticosa,* the box of Colonial gardens, grows less rapidly than *B. sempervirens.* In the North it is best suited for edging purposes; it also works out well wherever a low hedge is designated.

Among the other evergreens well adapted for hedges and enclosures, *Tsuga canadensis* (Hemlock) is one of the choicest selections to make. In growing a Hemlock hedge, it is best to prune it in such a way as to permit an ample supply of sunshine to reach all parts of the plants. For this reason the Gothic arch or triangular methods of training are best for this evergreen. As an enclosure to the flower garden, it gives a perfect background. Hemlocks grow well in the northern half of this country, and they thrive in soils that are fertile, moist, and well drained. *Ilex crenata* (Japanese Holly) and its variety *convexa* are also admirable. They are hardy, easy-to-grow, and most decorative. One of the upright growing varieties of *Taxus* (Yew), such as *Taxus Hicksii,* is just as satisfactory in point of hardiness and vigor as the Japanese Holly, and it has the advantage of growing faster than the Holly. In common with the Japanese Holly its rich, dark-green color remains practically unchanged all year round.

Living Fences.   A living fence is one which is more or less impenetrable and its principal function is to bar intruders from the garden. To achieve this particular objective, thorny plants must be used. *Rosa multiflora* and *Poncirus trifoliata,* commonly known as *Citrus trifoliata* or Hardy-orange, are well adapted for living fence purposes. In the North, if given a sheltered location, they will survive zero temperatures. The splendid foliage and brilliant berries of *Pyracantha coccinea* and its variety *Pyracantha coccinea Lalandi* (Firethorn) are known and loved by gardeners everywhere. The thorns of this shrub are sufficiently formidable for it to qualify for a living fence.

Topiary Work.   Topiary work consists of the shearing of woody ornamentals, mostly evergreens, into various kinds of unusual forms, such as birds, animals of all kinds, furniture, and in fact any shape that is unnatural to the normal habit of the shrub.

Shrubs intended for topiary work must from the beginning receive careful attention. Only those plants that are compact in their habit of growth are suitable for this use. Vigorous specimens must be obtained,

A simple example of topiary work is shown in the Yews each side of the porch entrance. Shrubs enhance the beauty of this all-yellow flower garden. *Mahonia* and *Berberis Julianae* are planted on the left. *Owners, Mr. and Mrs. Huston B. Almond. Courtesy Horticulture. Photographer, the Roches.*

and from the start clipping is necessary in order to establish and maintain a solid, compact growth. This pruning must be done at intervals during the growing season if good results are to be had.

Generally speaking, topiary work when done on a large scale is appropriate for use only in strictly formal gardens and on places where the conventionality of the various forms will fit in with the general planting and architectural scheme. However, the average home gardener who wants a touch of the unusual can introduce a moderate amount of topiary work.

Its association with gardens of the past gives this form of gardening a special interest to garden lovers of today. It is interesting to learn from the writings of Pliny the younger that his garden at his Tuscan villa contained all kinds of elaborate topiary work. "In front of the Portico is a sort of terrace, embellished with various figures, and bounded by a box hedge, from which you descend by an easy slope, adorned with the representation of diverse animals in box, answering alternately to each other; this is surrounded by a walk enclosed with tonsile evergreens shaped into a variety of forms." Again we read: "In one place you have a little meadow; in another the box is cut into a thousand different forms; sometimes into letters expressing the name of the master; sometimes that of the artificer; whilst here and there little obelisks rise intermixed alternately with fruit trees."

Topiary work has been practiced in European countries for centuries. It is thought that it was introduced into England by the Romans, and it is recorded as the custom of the times "for the nobilty to develop pleasure gardens in the orchards beyond the walls of their castles, the chief embellishment of which consisted in plants cut into monstrous figures, labyrinths, etc." In Italy and France the trimming was, on the whole, simpler in design. Many sheared hedges and Box-edged paths were combined with trees formal in their habit of growth. In France this art was practiced chiefly in obtaining the large and pretentious landscape effects that characterize the gardens of the latter Renaissance period. In the Colonial gardens of our own country the topiary work was executed on a less elaborate scale, such as clipped Box hedges in simpler forms, and parterre gardens edged with Box. Several of these Colonial gardens are still in existence, a noteworthy example being the Box garden at Mount Vernon.

Chapter IV

How to Propagate Your Own Shrubs

To watch a plant develop from the first stir of life until maturity is reached is one of the most fascinating of all garden adventures. It is surprising how easily even the uninitiated can propagate a number of the loveliest shrubs. The simplest methods of propagation are by layering, division, and cuttings. Many gardeners are especially intrigued by raising shrubs from seed; however interesting this may be, it is a slow, tedious procedure. In determining which kind of propagation to follow, you must consider the preference of the individual shrub.

Air-Layering. Layering is the process by which a plant can be propagated by rooting a branch while it is still attached to the parent plant; this can be done in various ways. Many shrubs can be increased by air-layering, and for the home gardener this is one of the easiest and most effective methods to employ, because larger plants can usually be produced in a shorter length of time than by any other procedure except division, which can be used only for certain shrubs. For centuries the Chinese have been proficient in this art, and for many years air-layering has been practiced in greenhouses and in tropical countries, where atmospheric conditions are conducive to root formation. However, since the introduction of polyethelene plastic, it is now possible to succeed with air-layers made outdoors in practically every climate.

Polyethelene plastic is sold under different trade names and comes already treated with hormones and fungicides. It retains moisture and has

Low-growing plants fill the beds at the pool level; this avoids blocking the upper level from view with its attractive shrubbery planting along the wood-woven fence. *Photographer, Gottscho-Schleisner.*

the valuable quality of allowing gases to escape. The actual process is of the simplest. Select a well-formed branch that is one or more years old, (The younger the wood, the more readily it will develop roots.) Care should be taken not to use a branch that will detract from the shapeliness of the parent bush. Remove all the leaves and twigs from the part to be layered; then make a cut on the branch in one of two ways. One method is called tonguing. With a sharp knife make a slicing cut one or two inches long down the branch at the point where the roots are to form; this cut is kept propped open with a small amount of moist sphagnum moss, and the bark is left intact. The second method is to remove a circle of bark at least half an inch wide from around the branch. In both instances the cut is made just below a node (joint), and the cut surfaces are *lightly* dusted with a hormone rooting powder. The object in making the wound is to diminish the flow of hormones, thus diverting strength into the development of roots. The whole layer is then covered with a generous handful of the moss so that the future roots will not be cramped. Before applying the moss, it is of utmost importance to squeeze out any excessive water so that it will be moist but not wet. Next, wrap the ball with an 8 x 10-inch sheet of the plastic, twist it at both ends, and tie these ends securely with Twist-ems, waterproof electrican's tape, or florist's plant tape. Wrap the plastic so that the overlap will be on the underside of the branch, to keep out the rain water.

Roots form sooner in cool weather; therefore the best time to make air-layers is in the early spring before the buds break, or in the late summer or fall. It takes from a few weeks to one or more years for the roots to develop, depending upon the age of the branch and the kind of shrub. Sometimes, but not always the new roots can be seen through the plastic; it is well to examine them in two or three months. With this method of propagation, no care is required until the new plant is severed from its parent. If the roots form late in the fall, the layer can remain on the parent plant until the following spring, which is a propitious time to sever it from its parent; at that season the weather is genial and warm, and the new plants will take hold and grow readily in their new quarters. Detach the new layer from its parent just below the ball of roots and allow some of the sphagnum moss to remain on it. Plant it in a shady spot with plenty of peat moss tucked in around the roots; keep the plant moist and the leaves sprinkled until new growth commences, which is the proof that the young shrub has become established. Great care of the plant at this time is a necessity; otherwise it will not survive.

Natural Layering. In nature, examples of natural layering are frequently found in shady or woodsy locations, where the falling leaves are left undisturbed year after year. The procumbent branches of many of our favorite shrubs eventually take root under the damp accumulation of leaf mold, which results from the decomposition of the leaves. Natural layering is especially prevalent among members of the Heath Family (Ericaceae). This important group of plants includes such popular bushes as Rhododendrons, Azaleas, Mountain-Laurel, Heather, Andromeda, Leucothoe, and Enkianthus.

Simple Layering. In simple layering the home gardener follows nature's example and supplies the layer with "ready-made" conditions which greatly accelerate the process of root growth. This and air-layering are the best methods for the amateur to practice. The shrubs which lend themselves most especially to all types of layering (with the exception of air-layering, which can be applied to any part of the top growth) are those with low, spreading branches which grow close enough to the ground to be easily bent and covered with soil. As in the case of air-layering, the best seasons for accomplishing the work are in early spring before growth commences, or in late summer when the wood has hardened.

In simple layering the first step is to prepare the soil where the layer is to be laid. This is done by mixing peat moss or leaf mold with sand and working it into the ground. The branch is then wounded (as in air-layering), the position of the cut being determined by the size of the branch; generally speaking, it is made a foot or so below the tip of the branch. The wound is made either by scraping the bark down to the wood or by tonguing (as described previously). It is best to make the cut on the upper surface of the branch as a precaution against breakage, which sometimes occurs when it is made on the underside of the stem. The wounded portion is then pegged into the well-prepared bed of mellow soil, and the branch is given a good twist at the wound so that its top will stand upright. Cover the layer with a mound of the prepared soil mixture, and support the branch in its vertical position with a stone, clod of earth, or a stake. On no account should any other part of the branch be covered with soil; the leaves must remain uncovered so that the normal functioning of the plant will not be interrupted.

Windows close to the ground call for low-growing plant material.
Courtesy Mahoney Construction Company. Photographer, Bill Harris.

In dry weather, watering will be required to prevent the layer from drying out; no fertilizer is needed because the layer draws its nutrients from the parent bush. The care of the new plant after it is severed from the shrub is identical to that described under air-layering.

The pendulous branches of some shrubs root so easily that it is only necessary to open a shallow trench a few inches deep, lay the tips in it, and cover them with fertile soil; then anchor them to the ground with stones, pegs, or soil clods.

Serpentine or Compound Layering.   Serpentine layering consists of pegging occasional parts of a flexible stem down to the ground and covering these with soil; the intervening parts are allowed to stand up in the air, forming arches.

Mound, Stool, or Hillock Layering.   This layering is accomplished by heavily pruning back the bush to within a few inches from the ground and covering it with a good pile of soil; this is done in spring. New shoots will begin to appear with roots of their own growing in the heaped up soil. When another spring comes around these rooted shoots can be separated and planted out.

Hardwood Cuttings.   Many shrubs can be grown from cuttings taken in the fall from ripened (dormant) wood. These are known as hardwood cuttings. Shoots of the current season's growth are especially desirable, because they root sooner than slips made from older wood. The stems are cut into lengths about six to ten inches, and are placed in boxes between layers of sphagnum moss or peat moss, these boxes are stored in a cool cellar, preferably in a temperature of forty to forty-five degrees. They should be watered from time to time in order to keep them *slightly* moist. When a cellar is available, cuttings can also be made in winter and given the same treatment. If a cool cellar is not available, the cuttings are tied together in bunches and buried heads up below the frost line. The bunches are completely covered with sphagnum moss, and the hole is then filled in with soil.

The cuttings may be planted outdoors in spring, but better rooting will take place if planting is deferred until the following fall. Before setting the cuttings out remove the lower buds, and plant so that the upper bud is just at the surface of the ground. They should be spaced four to eight inches apart.

Softwood Cuttings. Softwood cuttings are taken in spring from the growing wood. After the early flowering shrubs have finished blooming, and the annual pruning has been attended to, the prunings can be utilized for this purpose. The later blooming bushes may also be started from cuttings at this time, but the current season's flowering effect would be partly sacrificed (see page 27). The shoots that snap when bent are suitable for rooting, while those that crush or bend without breaking should be discarded. Make the cuttings three or four inches in length, or long enough for each slip to have from two to four nodes (joints). A smooth clean cut is made immediately below the bottom node. The lower leaves are removed from the cutting and the upper ones are retained; if the leaves are large, cut them in half to reduce loss of moisture through transpiration.

The use of a frame for planting cuttings is quite ideal, but most gardeners do not have this convenience. Cuttings can be rooted indoors in saucers filled with sand, which must be kept continually moist to ensure success. One of the plant propagator kits on the market comes equipped with a plastic cover and is excellent to use if only a few slips are to be made. Gardener's flats and shallow pots (bulb pans) are satisfactory alternatives. Whichever container is used, sufficient drainage must be provided by covering the bottom with broken pots or rubble. Over this, place a layer of well-firmed garden soil, filling the flat to within three or four inches of the top, which will allow space for a finishing layer of a rooting medium. Shredded sphagnum moss or vermiculite are excellent rooting mediums. If vermiculite is to be the medium, it should be watered several times a day before it is used, and sphagnum moss must be watered and well drained before planting the cuttings. If any other material is used, it should be sterilized as a precaution against disease (see page 52). The sphagnum moss and vermiculite are exceptions to the rule; they are already sterile.

The cut ends of the slips are lightly dusted with a hormone rooting powder and planted one inch deep and two or three inches apart. The cuttings should be shaded with newspapers to keep them from wilting, and they must be kept carefully watered by sprinkling the tops with a fine spray. On the other hand, one has to avoid over-watering, which would cause the stems to rot before they root. When the young plants become established and growth commences, they should be transplanted singly to two-inch pots containing good garden soil that is not too heavy. This will give the needed nourishment for the plants to draw upon for growth. Keep the pots cultivated and watered so that the cuttings will continue to grow along happily without a check. In sections where the winters are severe, ample protection is advisable to bring the young plants through the low temperatures.

If a frame is used, a three-inch layer of shredded sphagnum moss or vermiculite is spread over the surface soil. The cuttings are inserted in the medium to a depth of one inch; when the new roots grow, they will forage down into the soil for their food. In this instance, potting is unnecessary.

The newest treatment for rooting softwood cuttings is the "fog" treatment, which is being used to some extent commercially. In this treatment the cuttings are grown outdoors in a sunny location and kept constantly moist with a mist-like spray of water. Obviously, it may not be a practical method for the average home gardener. (For further details, write to The American Horticultural Society, Washington, D. C., for a copy of their January 1954 publication on "Vegetative Propagation.")

A clever practice of a gardener friend of mine is to buy rooted cuttings at a minimum cost. When these grow sufficiently, he increases the supply by taking cuttings from them; he roots them in a home-made frame which he constructed from discarded lumber, and for the sash he uses an old storm window. Another friend starts his cuttings outdoors under a mason jar that has a wide mouth; in the winter, he protects the jar with leaves or straw.

Root Cuttings.   Certain shrubs—such as Halesia, Vaccinium, Calycanthus, Aralia spinosa, and Chaenomeles—can be increased by root cuttings. These cuttings are made in the fall from roots that are about the thickness of a lead pencil; they are cut into pieces three or four inches long and are buried outdoors two or three inches deep in a horizontal position. A cool cellar is a satisfactory place to winter these cuttings, but they must not be allowed to dry out; they are put between layers of sphagnum moss in flats and stored. In the spring the cuttings are planted one or two inches deep outdoors. Dr. John L. Creech says: "With some plants, such as the Beach Plum, better results are obtained if the root pieces are inserted upright with the end exposed. Evidently the exposure to light exerts some influence on the initiation or growth of the adventitious buds."

Evergreens give a finishing touch to the ends of the wall. Placed each side of the stoop, they mark the entrance. *Photographer, Paul E. Genereux.*

Leaf Cuttings.   If one possesses a greenhouse, growing shrubs from leaves is made easier. The leaves are laid on the propagating bench with their undersides placed on a layer of shredded sphagnum moss. Little wooden pegs (toothpicks are convenient) are thrust through the main veins of the leaves to hold them in place. Rooting is encouraged at the points where the ribs have been wounded by pegging, and the small plants will emerge. Shading must be given, and the atmosphere should be kept moist and warm.

Division.   Shrubs are divided in much the same way that perennials are divided. A sharp spade is used to cut a clump of the bush into two or more parts. Shrubs such as Kerria, Mock-Orange, and Weigela, which grow many branches from the ground up, are adapted to this form of propagation. Each division should have its own roots intact and should be planted separately. Before planting, prune back all straggly roots and shorten the branches to encourage a stocky growth. The work can be done in spring or fall, spring being preferable in cold localities.

Suckers.   The advantage of increasing plants from suckers is the ease with which the work is done. The suckers are shoots that appear around the bush. These can be severed from the parent shrub with a portion of root attached. They can be planted in an out-of-the-way spot until they grow into well-shaped specimens. Of course, this method is restricted to the plants that sucker freely, such as the Lilac, Bayberry, and Mahonia.

Seeds.   Starting shrubs from seed is highly specialized procedure, and only the ardent plant propagator will have the patience and enthusiasm to increase his stock in this way. Seeds must be allowed to ripen before they are collected. The longevity of the specific seeds must be considered; in some cases it is necessary to sow them as soon as they are ripe, whereas others can be stored in a cool dry place for a certain length of time. (For information on this aspect of seeding, other than that given under the individual cultures, write to the U.S. Department of Agriculture.)

Select a well-drained location for the seed bed, or if this is not available, excavate the ground to the depth of at least one foot. Spread a one- or two-inch layer of some coarse material (such as the larger siftings of coal ashes) over the bottom of the excavation to provide adequate drainage; then refill with light, friable soil.

The first step to success in sowing seeds is to prepare the seed bed with care. When the soil is heavy, the upper three or four inches at least should be ameliorated by incorporating sand, compost, and peat moss in equal parts. The surface soil is raked into a fine tilth to facilitate germination. If the seeds to be sown are very tiny (the size of grains of pepper or a trifle larger), the top half-inch of soil should be sifted into an especially fine texture and the seeds sown directly on it; dust them over with just enough of the well-sifted soil to hide them from view; then press the seeds into close contact with the soil with a flat piece of wood.

The proper depth to sow larger seeds is approximately twice the diameter of the seed. Great care must be exercised to prevent the seeds from drying out—they should be kept watered with a fine spray; protection from the sun is of decided value and can be provided by driving stout stakes in the corners of the seed bed to support a covering of burlap or lath for the purpose.

If seeds are started indoors in flats or seed pans, they are safeguarded from the hazards of the weather. Adequate drainage is provided by placing over the bottom of the receptacles bits of broken pots or rubble before filling in with soil. The earth shoud be firmed and should come to within about three inches of the top; this will leave space for a finishing layer of shredded sphagnum moss or vermiculite. The seeds are broadcast, or sown in rows (drills) that are two inches apart. After they are sown, they are lightly syringed with water, and the receptacle is covered with a pane of glass or a plastic film, which in turn is covered with a piece of paper. The glass or plastic must be turned every day so that the moisture that collects on the underside will not drip on the soil; careful watering is necessary, but too much will be harmful. Germination takes place more rapidly if the newly sown seed is kept in a dark place. Immediately upon germination the covering is removed and the flats or pans placed in the full light; otherwise spindly seedings will result.

Sphagnum moss * grows in land that is acid and boggy. Since it absorbs and retains water to an unusual degree (it has an interesting water-retaining cellular formation), and in addition is a sterile medium, its use in plant propagation is particularly important.

Sphagnum moss contains some nutrition which helps the growth of seedlings until they are large enough to transplant. If they are grown in

* Farmer's Bulletin No. 2085 on Sphagnum Moss, U. S. Dep't of Agriculture.

the moss for some months, it is necessary to supply nourishment during the growing season. This is done by using a liquid fertilizer (according to directions) or a complete fertilizer such as a 10-6-4 in the proportion of two teaspoons to one gallon of water at monthly intervals.

Sphagnum moss must be shredded before it is used. Work it by hand through a screen which has three meshes to the inch. (The commercial grower will find a machine more practical.)

Sterilization.   Whether the seeds are to be started in the open or indoors, sterilization of the soil and the seeds is a prerequisite; this treatment has almost entirely conquered the dreaded damping-off fungus.

When only a small amount of soil is required, it can be sterilized with heat. The soil is made quite moist and then placed in an oven for one hour at a temperature of 180 degrees Fahrenheit. An alternative is to pour over the soil a generous amount of boiling water. Of course, in either case the soil must cool off entirely before seed is sown in it.

Another method used to sterilize soil is to treat it with formalin (this contains formaldehyde). The soil is heavily soaked with a solution of two teaspoons of formalin to four gallons of water; two weeks should elapse before sowing the seed. An added protection against damping-off is to spread over the sterilized soil a layer about one inch thick of shredded sphagnum moss or Vermiculite; as already mentioned, these two mediums are sterile. Unlike other substances, the Vermiculite should not be firmed down, but merely spread over the soil surface. Either of these mediums will provide an ideal seed bed.

Just before sowing, the seeds are sterilized by treating them with Zinc Oxide or any other of the seed disinfectants, such as Semesan or Arasan. The seedlings first develop seed leaves (cotyledons); then the true leaves that characterize the plant appear; when these achieve some growth, the time will be at hand to transplant the young seedlings. They must be faithfully watered, and for a week or more a little shade will be most beneficial.

Stratification.   The seeds of certain shrubs have to be stratified. Stratification is the process by which the hard outer covering of the seed is softened to assist germination. The most approved medium to use for stratification is shredded sphagnum moss. Prepare the flat with drainage and soil as previously described, using about three inches of firmed shredded sphagnum moss for the finishing layer; sow the seeds on the moss and lightly cover them with additional sphagnum moss. Keep the flat in a deep cold frame that is protected or is in a location that is above-freezing. The moss should be dampened before using, and it will not ordinarily require further watering. In most instances the seeds will sprout the first spring after being stratified. However, the length of time the seeds should be subjected to stratification is governed by the kind of seeds that are sown. This information can be obtained from the U. S. Department of Agriculture, or WOODY PLANT SEED MANUAL, prepared by the Forest Service, U.S.D.A., U. S. Gov. Printing Office, Washington 25, D. C.

Roses are ideal companions for the leisure hours. *Photographer, J. Horace McFarland Company.*

Chapter V

Roses Are Always Welcome

Enthusiasts throughout the centuries have shared the joy of growing roses. If you have never experienced this delight, by all means plan now to make a beginning, even if only with one plant! This queen of flowers —as it was called by Sappho—provides an ever-growing interest.

Roses have figured in religion, art, romance, and legend. In Greece they were held in high esteem. In the days of the Roman emperors, roses in abundance were used for all state occasions and private functions. A unique usage was that of covering the floors and the resting lounges at the great banquets with rose petals; huge sums were expended for this purpose. Rose petals were floated in wine glasses, and were also valued for medicinal purposes, for making scented oils, and for cooking. In the Middle Ages the gardens of the monasteries blossomed with their beauty; humble homes and noblemen's castles were gay with their presence. It was the Romans who first experimented with growing roses out of season by using pipes filled with hot water; this gave rise to today's extensive industry of growing roses under glass.

The Empress Josephine of France, with the assistance of the leading horticulturists and botanists of her day, sought to improve the rose, and to her goes the credit of giving the impetus to the hybridization still going on today. In her garden at Malmaison the Empress collected every type of rose that was then procurable—about 250 in all, as compared with the 5000 varieties that are now available. It appears that Napoleon shared Josephine's love of flowers, and his last night in France, before he departed for his exile to Elba, he spent in the beautiful garden at Malmaison. Indeed it was the Emperor who said: "Where flowers cannot be reared, there man cannot live!"

Roses are always cheerful garden companions, and they can be adapted to many uses. They are charming bordering a path or a terrace, and close to the front door they give a note of welcoming gaiety; combined with evergreens they are irresistible, and in the shrubbery border roses are always an addition. In fact, wherever a spot can be found that is sunny and well-drained—plant roses.

Different types of roses vary as to the amount of maintenance they require. For instance, there are many lovely shrub varieties which ask only for occasional fertilizing and an annual trimming to keep the bushes shapely. Other kinds of roses, such as Hybrid Teas and Floribundas, which are familiarly known as bedding varieties, require a certain amount of upkeep for maximum success.

Location.   Give your roses the sun they crave—at least six hours of it a day—and ample circulation of air; the latter is not only beneficial to the growth, but it also helps to prevent diseases. The ideal location is one in the full sun. In hot climates some shade from the burning afternoon sun is welcome. A windbreak, such as a house or a group of nearby trees, will shield the plants from severe north and northwest winds and will do much to prevent the canes from being lashed, broken, and loosened in the ground.

Where space is at a premium, ideal situations do not always exist. In many instances roses have to be tucked in close to hedges and shrubbery; the roots of these more stalwart growers compete seriously with the roses for food and water. This difficulty can be overcome in part by giving them extra fertilizer and more frequent watering.

A more efficient method, however, is to prevent the avid shrub roots from encroaching upon those of the roses. Separate the two by driving a sheet of metal vertically into the soil to a depth of two feet, or by building a concrete wall six inches thick, and extending two feet into the ground. These dividers need not protrude above ground. Dr. R. C. Allen in his excellent book *Roses for Every Garden* advises that roses should not be planted closer than "at least twenty feet away from large trees, six to eight feet from shrubs, and four feet from hedges." * Good drainage is an absolute essential; if water is absorbed soon after a heavy downpour, you can be reasonably sure the drainage is adequate. A more accurate test is to fill a hole eighteen inches deep with water; if the water disappears in a few hours, drainage will be no problem.

Soil Preparation. Expert rose growers now agree that the elaborate soil preparation which was formerly practiced is unnecessary. Any average garden soil that will grow vegetables or flowers satisfactorily will produce good roses with little previous preparation. This certainly simplifies rose-growing immeasurably and makes it possible for many more home-owners to include roses in their garden scheme.

If your soil is naturally fertile, you will only need to apply a generous layer (one or two inches thick) of organic matter over the surface of the soil and spade it under to the depth of a spading fork. This organic matter can be either peat moss or well-rotted cow manure, or better still, a combination of both; if leaf mold is available, it can be used instead of peat moss. A light dusting of superphosphate stirred into the soil will give the roses a good start. If your place is newly built, the chances are that there will be only a thin surface layer of topsoil; in this case remove the soil to the depth of ten or twelve inches and work a layer of the organic matter mentioned above into the bottom of the excavation. Refill the bed with a mixture of the same organic matter, using one spadeful to every four spadefuls of topsoil. Again a light application of superphosphate spread over the finished bed will be beneficial. If possible, give the soil at least two weeks to settle before you plant. Roses prefer soil that is slightly acid. To determine the degree of acidity of your soil, have a sample tested by your local County Agricultural Agent; the correct "range" is from pH 5,5 to pH 6,5. If the soil is too alkaline, it is apt to produce leaves that are mottled. This can be overcome by using

* Courtesy of M. Barrows and Company and Dr. R. C. Allen.

sulphur, peat moss, or some other acid-producing material. If the soil is too acid, it can be corrected with lime. Ordinarily this should be spread so as to appear like a light snowfall; it is applied in the fall, winter, or earliest spring; 1½ pounds of ground limestone to every 50 feet of ground is a good allowance.

There are two other essentials for successful rose culture: purchase good plants, and plant correctly. If field-grown, two-year-old, number-one-grade bushes are bought from a reliable rose grower, you will have the assurance that the plants will be well grown and will reach you in good condition.

As soon as the shipment is received, open the package to make sure that the packing material is moist. If it is dry, sprinkle it with water, but be careful not to wet it excessively. The sooner the plants are set out in the garden, the better it will be for their welfare. But if you cannot set them out at once, examine the packing every few days and carefully replace the covering. Be sure to store the package in a cool place. If planting is delayed for as long as a week, the bushes should be buried in the ground to keep the tops and the roots from drying out.

Planting.   The best time to plant roses differs with climatic conditions; for example, in the South the winter is preferable; in extremely cold regions spring is the safest season; and in moderately cold sections of the country roses can be planted either in the fall or in the spring. Planting distances also vary according to the location. On the Pacific Coast where growth is lusty, more space between the bushes must be allowed. Generally speaking, three feet apart is about right for Hybrid Teas, while in colder sections of the country, eighteen to twenty-four inches between the plants will be sufficient. Polyantha and Floribunda roses are planted from twelve to twenty-four inches apart, depending upon climate and variety; the same considerations determine the distance between shrub roses; this varies from four to eight feet apart.

The roots of roses dry out unbelievably fast when they are exposed to air and sun; therefore while planting is in progress it is a good idea to plunge two or three bushes at a time in a bucket of water, keeping the rest of the plants well covered in their package. Cut off all bruised, dead, or broken roots, and make the planting hole deep and wide enough to accommodate the roots comfortably, so that they will fall in their natural position without being twisted or cramped.

Loosen the soil in the bottom of the hole and remove any stones, as these only hamper growth. A little extra trouble taken at planting time will repay you amply with better roses throughout the years. In the center of the planting hole, place a small hill of soil on which to stand the bush.

The correct depth to plant varies with the different sections of the country. Where the winters are very severe, the bud (recognized as a knob-like protrusion on the stem above the roots) should be set two inches below the ground level; in moderately cold sections a covering of one inch will be sufficient; whereas in mild regions the bud should be just below or slightly above the surface level. When planting, throw into the hole only a small amount at a time of well-pulverized soil or compost, in order to work it firmly around and between the roots. Be careful that no interstices are left which would cause the roots to dry out. When the hole is about three-quarters full of soil, fill it with water; when the water has been absorbed, finish filling the hole with soil to ground level, or slightly above to allow for settling.

Dormant plants ordered from nurserymen are usually pruned to the proper height. If this is not the case, cut back the canes to twelve or fourteen inches from the ground. If dormant plants are planted in the spring, a mound of soil three or four inches high should be placed around the base of the canes to help soften the wood and to encourage the buds to break, which they will do in two or three weeks. Just as soon as this occurs, the soil mound must be removed gently, so as not to break the young growth.

Plants started in Ferto-Pots or cans are also available for spring planting. If these are set out carefully, the roots will not be disturbed and growth will not be checked to any appreciable degree.

Pruning. Formerly pruning was confusing to the amateur because different directions were given for each class of rose, and severe cutting was the order of the day. This practice has entirely changed, and the drastic pruning that used to be recommended is now considered injudicious.

The time to prune roses differs with the locality. The work is best done as soon as the buds begin to swell and after the danger of severe frost has passed. For northern gardeners this will be from March to mid-April, depending on the location. Southern gardeners will prune

Few realize that climbing Roses can be turned into bushes by careful pruning. This Silver Moon lends itself well to this treatment. *Photographer, the Roches.*

their roses during the winter from December to February, the exact time differing with the particular area. Shrub roses are pruned immediately after bloom; old woody canes should be removed at the base, and the straggly shoots and lateral growths shortened back enough to encourage a stocky growth.

A sharp pair of pruning shears will facilitate the work and prevent shaggy cuts that take more sap to heal and are more subject to disease. Make a slanting cut a quarter of an inch above the bud. Whenever possible, cut to a bud which points in an outward direction in order to direct the future growth in an outward instead of an inward direction.

We prune roses to make them shapely, to remove dead, diseased and weak wood, as well as canes that cross and rub each other. Cut out all twiggy growth; it only draws unnecessarily on the energy of the plant. Roses that are allowed to grow at will become straggly and ungainly; their appearance can be greatly improved by an annual "grooming." All healthy canes should be kept, and cut to a more-or-less uniform height to twelve to twenty-four inches, according to the objective of the pruner. Naturally, bigger bushes produce more flowers, but the blooms will not be so large. In climates where the growing season is long, roses are not cut so low.

Tree roses need more drastic pruning to maintain a well-formed top growth. Shorten the branches back to eight to ten inches from the main stem, and during the summer trim any long shoots that develop, so as to keep the plants symmetrical.

Climbing roses are pruned immediately after flowering. Ramblers, as their name implies, spread prodigiously unless they are kept within bounds. New canes spring up rapidly during the summer; therefore remove those that have flowered to make room for the newcomers. The large-flowered varieties, which bloom intermittently all summer long, are not such prolific growers. These only need to have the laterals (side shoots) shortened back to about four inches from the main stem. As the new canes appear, the old woody ones can be removed at the base. In spring the only pruning required will be to take away the dead wood, and do a little nipping back here and there to give a trim appearance.

Routine Care.   The upkeep of roses is essentially similar to that of perennials and annuals. Keep the soil cultivated, water the ground whenever necessary, plan and carry out a regular program of spraying or dusting. Roses have shallow feeding roots; so it is very harmful to work the ground deeply, especially during the height of the growing season. Simply stir the earth enough to maintain a loose soil mulch.

Watering should be thorough; otherwise it will do more harm than good. A light watering will attract the roots to the surface where they will suffer from drought and be more susceptible to winter injury. Soak the ground to a depth of six or eight inches; this is a very important part of the upkeep, and if attended to regularly throughout the season will do much to keep the bushes vigorous and blooming steadily. Do not water the foliage late in the day. Roses should go to bed with dry leaves, since wet foliage at night invites disease.

A summer mulch about one to one and a half inches deep of peat moss or buckwheat hulls greatly reduces the weeding, helps to keep the roots cool, conserves moisture, and adds to the neat, smart appearance of the bed. Peat moss is excellent and good for the soil, though buckwheat hulls are preferred by some gardeners because they are light and easy to handle. The roses in my garden are always mulched with peat moss, which is applied before the June bloom. It dresses up the garden and makes the flowers appear at their best. It is done after a heavy rainfall. If there is no rain, the beds are watered thoroughly and the surface soil is stirred as soon as it is dry enough to be worked; then the mulch is spread. Buy your peat moss in early spring and let it stand outdoors where the spring rains will moisten and soften it; dry peat moss is lumpy and more difficult to apply.

An all-purpose spray or dust must be diligently used at weekly intervals throughout the season, or more often if there is frequent rainfall. Commence with this program in spring when the new growth is three or four inches long, the objective being to prevent rather than to cure diseases. Complete coverage of stems, under surfaces as well as upper surfaces of leaves, is absolutely essential for complete protection. Tri-Ogen, or one of the dusts offered by one of the large rose-growing establishments, is dependable. New chemicals are constantly being introduced, and the important companies keep pace with the times and change their formulas accordingly. For control of black spot, the rose expert Mr. Richard Thomson advises using a dormant spray early in March of four tablespoons of Captan to one gallon of water, plus two drops (using a medi-

Roses and Box border the brick walk, and Yews and Japanese Holly soften the house line; *Pieris japonica* accents each side of the front door. *Photographer, Paul E. Genereux.*

cine dropper) of a spreader sticker. When the new shoots are about one inch long, spray again with a weaker solution, using two tablespoons of Captan to one gallon of water and two drops of the spreader sticker; this spray should be applied every week throughout the season. It can be used in the hottest weather without danger of foliage damage. To combat mildew, the best preparation is Mildex, but it cannot be used unless the temperature is below 80 degrees. Great care must be taken to follow the manufacturer's directions meticulously.

Fertilizers. Actually, roses do not require a great deal of feeding— in fact, harm is sometimes done by over-fertilizing. After the winter protection is removed, an application of well-rotted cow manure is excellent. It provides fertility and organic matter to the soil; work it into the ground very lightly with a spading fork, and be careful that the manure does not touch the canes. This advice holds good for whatever fertilizer is used. If manure is not applied, substitute a good commercial fertilizer, either a 4-12-4 or a 5-10-5, when the young growth is approximately four inches in length. Follow the manufacturer's directions as to quantity and spread the fertilizer evenly around the plants. Some gardeners recommend a second feeding just before the June bloom; however, my roses are fertilized the second time immediately after the flowers have faded; and in early August (no later than August 15) they receive their final feeding for the season. Rake the fertilizer lightly into the soil, and if rain is not imminent, water it into the ground. A foliar feeding, such as Ra-Pid-Gro, can be used instead of the kinds applied to the soil; it is simple to use and especially convenient after the plants have been covered with their summer mulch.

Propagation. Roses are propagated by seed, budding, grafting, layering, division, and cuttings. The home gardener will do well to increase his supply by layers or cuttings. Division is also an easy, worthwhile method, but it is restricted to the varieties that have a clump-like habit of growth, such as the shrub varieties. Cuttings can be readily rooted outdoors under a glass jar which has a wide opening, and they are best taken from firm, healthy flowering wood a few days after the bloom has faded. The faded flower is removed, the slips are made about eight inches long, and the base of the cutting should be made immediately below a leaf. The lower leaves are removed, leaving the top two or three leaflets intact.

Plant the cutting in a shady location, in friable soil mixed with peat moss, and set it into the ground to within a couple of inches from its top leaflets. The soil should be kept moist at all times; however, with the protection of the glass jar it is usually unnecessary to water often unless the weather is excessively dry. The slip usually roots in a month or six weeks. When it has rooted and the cutting begins to grow, remove the jar and give the young plant an ample covering for winter protection. If by any chance the roots have not formed by the fall, leave the glass jar over the cutting, and heap leaves or straw over it to carry it through the cold months.

For layering, see directions for Simple Layering on page 44.

Winter Protection. In November after a severe frost, protect the roses with a six- or eight-inch mound of earth placed around each plant; this will keep them from being heaved up by the alternate action of freezing and thawing. For this purpose, when the roses are closely planted, it is best to use soil from a source other than the rose bed itself, such as the compost pile, or wherever good soil can be found. If the soil is taken from the rose bed, it leaves the roots of the bushes without adequate covering, which is much needed to bring them safely through the winter months; also it will inevitably destroy some of the valuable roots.

If you live where the winters are extraordinarily severe and the temperatures usually drop below zero, additional protection of salt hay or evergreen boughs is advisable. Tree roses are not so easy to protect, nor can they stand as much cold as Hybrid Teas and Floribundas. In the North, part of the root system should be loosened from the ground so that the plant can be laid in a trench and covered with soil; then it should be further protected with salt hay or evergreen boughs.

Never use leaves for winter protection for roses; they hold too much moisture and frequently cause winter killing by becoming packed and water-logged. Cut back any long canes to about two and a half to three feet in length; this will prevent them from being whipped by high winds which may loosen them in the ground.

Old-Time Roses. Varieties of roses come and go, every year bringing new and tempting kinds in gorgeous colors and larger and still larger blooms. Much as we may love these and depend on Hybrid Teas and Floribundas for our chief rose garden display, we should not allow their glamour completely to obscure the delicate beauty and delicious fra-

Well-placed evergreens provide contrast in height, texture and color to the flower border. A compact hedge gives background to the rose bed. *Photographer, Paul E. Genereux.*

grance of the old-time shrub roses. Fortunately, these are again coming into favor; they are rich in historic interest and bring into the garden a note of distinction and background. Plant one of these bushes near a window or doorway where the gentle breezes will carry its sweet scent indoors. In a perennial border, a shrubbery planting, in softening a wall, or wherever a bare sunny spot needs to be brought to life, these bushes with their gay flowers will contribute a charm of their own. The brightly colored fruits which follow the blossoms are also of decorative value, frequently persisting on the branches throughout the winter months. Shrub roses are hardy and easy to grow, and they are less susceptible to insects and diseases than the other kinds. They will grow in practically any garden soil, provided it is not too sandy. They are easily transplanted in fall or spring and require no special attention once they are fully established—just a little annual pruning. (Directions for pruning roses are given under Pruning earlier in this chapter.)

Species Roses.   There are various kinds of species roses from which to make a selection, but none as fragrant as the Damask Rose (*R. damascena*, Zone IV). The Cabbage Rose (*R. centifolia*, Zone V), the old rose of Provence, and the French (*R. Gallica*, Zone V) also bring their sweet scent to the garden. The Moss Rose (*R. centifolia muscosa*) is another lovely kind to include, as is the Scotch Rose. The latter is a descendant of *R. spinossisima*, Zone IV; a popular member of this group is Harison's Yellow. These are all outstanding representatives of the unforgettable old-fashioned roses.

Among other roses of garden interest for use as shrubs or for informal hedges are the following:

R. blanda, Zone II?, Meadow Rose, produces pale pink flowers; it is an upright-growing shrub with red stems.

R. carolina, Zone IV, has pink flowers, red fruit (hips), good foliage effect, and a pleasing, spreading habit of growth. This desirable rose is well adapted for hedges three to five feet in height.

R. chinensis, Zone VII?, China Rose, is not hardy in the far North; its colors range from white to pink and red. This species is the ancestor of many of today's roses.

R. cinnamomea, Zone IV, Cinnamon Rose, produces delightfully fragrant deep pink flowers; it grows into a bush about seven feet tall.

R. Eglanteria, Zone IV, (*R. rubiginosa*), Sweet-brier rose, is the ancestor of the lovely bush roses known as Penzance Briers. The foliage of most of the varieties is fragrant when wet. The flowers come in shades of pink and red. This shrub can be kept compact with proper pruning.

R. *foetida,* Zone IV, (R. *lutea*), which has been a garden inhabitant for three centuries, is an ancestor of the Austrian Briers. Desirable varieties of this species are Austrian Yellow and Persian Yellow. Unfortunately, R. *foetida* is especially subject to black spot and should not be planted close to other roses.

R. *multiflora,* Zone V, Japanese Rose, bears clusters of white flowers in early June. It is a vigorous, hardy species with arching branches. It is frequently used for living fences because of its thorny branches and thick growth. Severe and repeated pruning is necessary to keep this rampant grower within bounds.

R. *nitida,* Zone III, Shining Rose, is a hardy dwarf species that grows less than two feet high. It has deep pink flowers and glossy foliage.

R. *palustris,* Zone IV, will grow in swampy ground where planting is usually a problem. This rose grows about eight feet tall, and the attractive pink flowers give color over quite an extended period.

R. *rubrifolia,* Zone II, Red-leaf Rose, is an unusual species because of its dark, reddish leaves and small, deep-pink, star-shaped flowers. It grows into a shrub approximately six feet tall and is sometimes used to give contrast in color of foliage.

R. *setigera,* Zone IV, Prairie Rose, develops into a large shrub with graceful branches. The pink flowers appear in mid-summer after most roses have finished blooming.

R. *virginiana,* Zone III, (R. *lucida*), Virginia Rose, has glossy foliage and bright pink, pale pink, or white flowers, which are followed by ornamental red fruit (hips).

R. *Wichuriana,* Zone V, Memorial Rose, is trailing in its habit of growth. Its branches travel along the ground and strike root, spreading over a large area. Because of this, it is splendid for covering sunny banks and slopes. Its fragrant white flowers and lustrous leaves give a lovely effect.

Rosa Hugonis, Zone V, Father Hugo Rose, is much loved for its wealth of soft yellow flowers that cover the pendulous branches in May. Pruning will help to keep the plant shapely. Apart from the beauty of its flowers, it has the great advantage of thriving in poor soil.

Rosa rugosa, Zone II, the Hybrid Rugosa roses make excellent borders and hedges. The Hybrids are far superior to the old-time *Rosa rugosa.* A trailing variety, Max Graf, is useful for covering banks and slopes. Its sweet fragrance is especially enjoyable in the dampness of the summer evening. The single, bright pink flowers show off admirably in the glossy green setting of its leaves.

Recent varieties of shrub roses which bloom intermittently through the summer can be procured, and these are delightful introductions for any garden.

Hybrid Perpetuals. Very popular at the turn of the century, the Hybrid Perpetual is not seen in many of today's gardens. This rose belongs preeminently to the month of June, at which time it blooms profusely. Only a few scattered flowers are produced during the summer and fall seasons, and this may account in part for its loss of popularity. Mr. Richard Thomson tells how it can be treated to induce bloom in mid-summer and again in the fall. The method is to fertilize heavily, water thoroughly whenever needed, and prune immediately after the June bloom. The recommended trimming is to shorten the lateral (side) shoots to two buds from the main stems. After the summer bloom, repeat the pruning and fertilizing. Never allow the plants to suffer from drought; this is an important cultural point to observe for flower production. Feed the plants again when the autumn bloom has ended. Fall feeding of Hybrid Perpetuals is not risky because the wood is hard enough to stand the winter temperatures. As previously mentioned, other kinds of roses should not be fertilized after August 15, because a soft growth would be induced that is likely to winter-kill.

For the collector of old-fashioned roses, Hybrid Perpetuals should have an important place. They can be used as bedding roses and kept to a height of about three feet, or they can be trained as shrubs and allowed to grow five or six feet tall. Frau Karl Druschki is the leading variety; its large, white, beautifully formed flowers make it outstanding in this class of roses.

Miniature Roses. These roses grow about six to twelve inches tall; they are dainty, charming little plants for the rock garden, for planting at the base of sun dials or bird baths, and for edging rose borders. Attractive varieties come in shades of pink, red, yellow, and white.

Part II

EVERGREENS FOR ALL-YEAR-ROUND EFFECT

Chapter VI

Evergreens—A through E

Evergreens are the mainstay of the all-year-round garden, since in most parts of the country their foliage effect is dependable for every month of the year. This group of plants contributes substantially to the solidarity of the planting; evergreens are the "old faithfuls," the permanent landmarks of that important bit of land called home. These plants, with their different shades of green and various textures and forms, offer interest and contrast even if used by themselves. Unlike the deciduous shrubs that shed their leaves in fall, the evergreens provide their welcome green touch to the winter landscape.

Evergreens are reliable standbys in so many ways—for background plantings, for enclosures to outdoor living areas, for foundation plantings, as screens for the drying yard or other unsightly spots. The pages that follow describe many of the leading types from which you can choose.

Generally speaking, broad-leaved evergreens are by nature inhabitants of milder climates. In this respect they differ from deciduous plants, which for the most part are more tolerant of lower temperatures. Indeed, some of the broad-leaved varieties are truly ever-green only in the gentler climates, becoming deciduous in the very cold winters of the North; in some sections where the temperatures are extremely low, they fail to survive.

73

The gate opens on to a stretch of lawn that is bordered with *Rhododendrons, Azaleas* and Laurels. An occasional Hemlock sharply breaks the planting line. *Owner, Miss Anne J. Pugh. Courtesy The American Home. Photographer, the Roches.*

Sloping ground offered an opportunity for a two-level garden in this small suburban property. In this instance the lower-level has been developed into a charming and intimate living area. *Owner, Miss Anne J. Pugh. Courtesy The American Home. Photographer, the Roches.*

The methods of propagation best suited to the individual shrubs are given under each culture. "How-to" directions are on pages 41–53.

Aucuba Japonica, Zone VII, Japanese Aucuba, is a highly ornamental plant with broad, glossy, dark-green leaves, growing from five to fifteen feet in height. In mild climates it is a valuable shrub to include in foundation plantings. Aucuba is not reliably hardy north of Washington, D. C.; however, it will grow in protected locations as far north as Philadelphia. In cold climates it can be successfully grown in tubs for patio and terrace decoration in summer and carried through the winter in a cool temperature indoors. During the growing season, *Aucuba* should be kept moist; but when it is brought indoors, it is best to keep it rather dry.

Aucuba flourishes in shade or in partial shade, and it likes rich, well-drained soil. Each spring the tips of the shoots should be trimmed back, and the old canes should be removed during the summer. One of its good qualities is its ability to endure unfavorable conditions of smoke and dust. Aucuba can be propagated by seeds or by softwood cuttings that are rooted under glass or in a shaded frame. The cuttings can also be grown in pots filled with sphagnum moss or peat moss. Keep the pots either in the house or in a shady spot outdoors until they are rooted. If the cuttings show signs of wilting, cover them with a Polythelene plastic bag supported by two or three stakes. Aucuba produces showy red berries, provided male and female plants are set out.

There are different varieties on the market, but by far the most attractive are those with solid green leaves. Although the variety *A. japonica variegata,* Gold Dust Tree, is the most generally planted, it is not an attractive form because its leaves are mottled yellow.

Berberis, Barberry, is easily grown. (For its requirements see page 153.) Although the majority of the species are deciduous, there are a few lovely evergreen kinds, the best of which are given below.

B. buxifolia, Zone (V), Magellan Barberry, comes to us from Chile; it is an upright-growing form and reaches a height of about ten feet. Lower-growing varieties of this species are *pygmaea* (three feet) and its variety *nana,* which is a dwarf and dense shrub. It is useful for foundation plantings as far north as Philadelphia. The taller type can be used in background planting, and the dwarfer kinds as facers.

B. Darwinii, Zone VII?, Darwin Barberry, is also a species from Chile; it is a particularly desirable kind with yellow flowers borne in clusters,

The upper-level is held by a stone retaining wall. The bed above this wall is planted with *Azaleas* and Green Island Holly; *Taxus repandens* accent each corner, and Periwinkle carpets the bed. A brick walk intersects this bed and the border on the right, which runs along the boundary wall of the property; this has been planted with *Rhododendrons, Azaleas, Pieris japonica* and Hemlocks. The double brick edging of the border has proved successful in preventing the soil from washing onto the brick walk. *Owner, Miss Anne J. Pugh. Courtesy The American Home. Photographer, the Roches.*

and the foliage is a lustrous green. It is definitely suited only to mild climates as it will not tolerate much frost.

B. Julianae, Zone (V), Wintergreen Barberry, is a handsome bush that attains a height of six feet. A plant of this species that has been kept compact by regular pruning develops into a splendid shrub for use as a specimen and for a hedge; it is also excellent in foundation plantings and in a mixed grouping of evergreen and deciduous shrubs.

B. Sargentiana, Zone VI?, Sargent Barberry, is an introduction from China; it is another attractive evergreen species and comes into its own wherever a shrub about six feet high is required.

B. triacanthophora, Zone V, Threespine Barberry, which grows to a height of three or four feet, has narrow leaves and spreading, graceful branches. The ivory white flowers are followed by blue-black berries. This shrub is a good hedge plant.

B. verruculosa, Zone (V), Warty Barberry, forms an exceptionally compact, dense, low shrub that is valuable for rock gardens or for accent plants on each side of a doorway; in fact, it is adapted to various garden uses because of its attractive foliage and habit of growth. Its small glossy leaves resemble those of a holly in miniature.

Buxus, Box is intimately associated with the gardens of the past and is a real aristocrat among the evergreens. Throughout the ages it has decorated countless gardens both large and small. During the reign of Louis XVI it was grown in the lavish gardens at Versailles, and in our own country it was introduced by the early settlers. Those valiant men and women who came to the New World, shorn of many of their possessions, brought seeds and cuttings from their native land, and among these were slips of their much treasured Box. What other plant will bring into the garden more vividly the memories of the box-edged flower borders of long ago? In Alice Morse Earle's *Old-Time Gardens* we read: "Over these old garden borders hangs literally an atmosphere of the past; the bitter perfume stimulates the imagination as we walk by the side of these splendid box bushes, and think, as every one must, of what they have seen, of what they know." *

---

* Alice Morse Earle, *Old-Time Gardens,* copyright 1901, used with the permission of The Macmillan Company.

Before the planting was made. *Photographer, Caryl R. Firth.*

A planting of Box is in keeping with the simple lines of this Maryland home. In climates where Box does not thrive, *Ilex crenata convexa* is a good substitute. *Owners, Mr. and Mrs. Thomas T. Firth. Photographer, Caryl R. Firth.*

Box thrives in a variety of soils, but prefers a friable, fertile one that is generously supplied with organic matter; peat moss or leaf mold worked into the ground will provide this requisite. Good drainage is one of the most important considerations in growing Box. It will grow best where there is shade for part of the day, although it will tolerate a sunny exposure. In transplanting, it should be set the same depth as it stood before —definitely not any deeper; in this respect it differs from most evergreens which like to be planted slightly deeper.

Pruning Box is largely a matter of individual taste. It should be done in early spring before the growth starts, and it merely consists of cutting back the tips of the shoots here and there to increase the vigor and compactness of the bush.

A mulch of peat moss through the summer months is very acceptable. If your Box requires feeding, an excellent formula consists of one part Cottonseed Meal, one part Bone Meal, to two parts of a 5-10-5 fertilizer. Spread the mixture in earliest spring around the outer reach of the roots (this is about in line with the outer spread of the top growth), using a trowelful of the fertilizer to a bush that measures more or less eighteen inches in each direction. Keep the plants well watered during the hot weather so that the growth will not be checked.

It is easy to increase your supply of Box by taking cuttings either before growth starts in the spring, or later in the season when the new growth has hardened.

In the cold sections of the country, winter covering is advisable unless the shrubs are growing in a well-protected situation (see page 31). In localities where there are snowstorms it pays to remove the snow in order to prevent breakage.

Box falls prey to various enemies for which the best preventive measures are to brush out any dead leaves, remove yellow foliage, and keep the dead wood cut out. For Box leaf miner, spray with Malathion when the adult flies commerce to emerge. The exact time varies with weather conditions. Usually the flies appear in early May, and from that time on, successive sprayings will be required after each rain for at least three weeks. Malathion is preferable to DDT because it does not have the mite build-up that unfortunately occurs with DDT. Malathion also comes into its own for use against red spider mites, those tiny insects that can be seen with the aid of a hand lens. They look like minute

Buxus microphylla, Korean Box, is of great value to the garden-maker because of its hardiness and dwarf habit. *Photographer, the Roches.*

grains of red pepper and they inhabit the undersides of the leaves. Soaking the foliage with water in the late afternoon is also helpful. The soft scale mealybugs that resemble bits of cotton also succumb to repeated sprayings of Malathion through the growing season, but to be effective, the applications must be heavy and thorough. They can also be attacked by using an oil spray, such as Volck, in earliest spring before growth starts; oil sprays should never be used on Box in warm or hot weather.

Box is very versatile in its uses; it can be introduced in almost every part of the planting scheme, such as bordering flower beds, walks, and drives. It is of great value for specimens, foundation plantings, accent points, hedges, and for topiary work.

This *Camellia japonica* has bloomed every April for the past ten years at Yonkers, N.Y. *Courtesy Boyce Thompson Institute. Photographer, Boyce Thompson Inst.*

B. microphylla var. koreana, Zone IV, Korean Box, is the hardiest form. Its dwarf habit of growth (two feet) makes it useful for planting in rock gardens and under the low windows of modern houses.

B. sempervirens, Zone (V), VI, Common Box, grows more rapidly than other forms and has a more open habit of growth; its variety *arborescens,* Tree Box, is considered by many to be the more interesting kind. Its tree-like, graceful form makes it especially well adapted for specimen planting. The variety *rotundifolia* grows into a rounded bush and is somewhat hardier than most kinds. *B. sempervirens var. myrtifolia,* Myrtle-leaved Box, is an attractive low-growing, narrow-leaved variety.

B. sempervirens var. suffruticosa, Dwarf Box, is the familiar slow-growing Box of old-time gardens. When allowed to grow unpruned, the shrubs assume billowy, irregular shapes which add to their charm and artistic effect.

Calluna Vulgaris (see page 156).

Camellia Japonica, Zone VII?, is treasured by garden lovers everywhere; in flower it is unusually decorative, and throughout the year its glossy, dark-green leaves and symmetrical form have won it well-deserved popularity.

Camellias do not thrive in climates that are hot all year round, but prefer being cool in winter; in fact, they have been known to survive temperatures close to zero, and they will usually withstand temperatures of 15 to 20 degrees above zero. The popularity of this lovely plant is rapidly spreading, and Northern gardeners who are intrigued with its beauty are experimenting with its culture outdoors as well as indoors. In sections of the country where the winters are really severe, tub or pot culture must be resorted to. Throughout the summer these potted plants add a note of distinction to a partly shady spot or to the patio or terrace. During the winter they are moved indoors to a sun parlor, greenhouse, or any cool place where the temperature is about 45 degrees at night and 50 degrees during the day. Raising Camellias outside of their climatic range is a challenge to one's gardening ability, and growing requirements under such conditions must be very strictly observed. A healthy, well-nourished, carefully tended plant stands a much better chance of coping with weather conditions not naturally suited to its well-being. It is important to keep snow brushed off the plants.

Among the hardier varieties of *Camellia japonica,* Dr. P. W. Zimmerman recommends *C. japonica Elegans* (*Chandler*) and *C. Kumasaka* (Lady Marion), both of which have been grown successfully at Yonkers, New York. They are worthy of special mention because they have withstood weather condtions and locations in both sun and shade. These varieties bloom early each spring and lend themselves well to landscape purposes; they are also recommended for use as cut flowers.

At the Boyce Thompson Institute for Plant Research at Yonkers, with which Dr. Zimmerman is associated, the hardy collection of seedlings— as yet unnamed—is of much interest. There is real promise that Camellias hardy enough for cold regions will result from experiments now taking place.

Camellias like a partly shady location, and they require an acid soil that is mellow and well mixed with organic matter. If the earth is not fertile, replace it with a mixture of rich topsoil, peat moss, and well-rotted cow manure in equal parts, to which is added a little commercial fertilizer. The plants are best set the same depth as they stood before. Immediately around the roots, work in some good soil, preferably compost, and firm it well. The planting hole is then filled in with the soil combination recommended above. For at least eight weeks after planting, the ground should be kept moist, and the tops of the plants should be sprinkled with water every other day. This care will do much to establish them and to give them a good start. Do not let the Camellias suffer at any time from drought, and when watering, bear in mind that they also like to have their leaves syringed. Another helpful growing hint is to keep the plants mulched with peat moss or leaf mold.

The needed nutrients in the soil should be maintained with two spring feedings annually. The first should be applied early in the season just before growth commences, the second one month later, but not after May first. One of the fertilizers on the market for acid-loving plants can be used and applied according to the manufacturer's directions. In summer, if the plants appear to need a little pick-up, give them an application of superphosphates combined with sulphate of potash in the proportion of five parts of the former to one part of the latter. Avoid the use of nitrogenous fertilizer at that season, because this would encourage new growth that would not have time to harden before frost. Whenever a fertilizer is used, it should be applied around the plant as far as the outer spread of its branches.

Propagation is done by seeds sown when ripe, by cuttings taken in mid-summer, and by layers.

Camellias have various uses. Planted as specimens they are especially fine; on each side of a doorway and to soften walls or house corners they are also effective. Camellias can also be used for background plantings and for espalier work. In cold climates the protection of the house wall is especially welcome. The *Sasanqua species,* Zone VII?, of which there are numerous varieties, is well suited for hedges.

Chamaecyparis, Retinispora, Retinospora, is a valuable evergreen which comes to us from Japan; it provides a wide range in height, from tree form to the lower-growing shrub-like type. The supply can be increased by cuttings. As accent plants they stand out dominantly, and well-grown stock can be used as specimens. *C. obtusa nana* can eventually attain a height of about ten feet and is well adapted for use as a hedge, as is also *C. obtusa compacta,* which grows to approximately six to ten feet.

Chamaedaphne Calyculata, Zone II, Leather-leaf, is a very desirable hardy evergreen shrub about three feet in height. It bears attractive racemes of white flowers in early spring. This shrub is excellent for use in foreground plantings and for accent purposes in the rock garden. A moist, light soil well supplied with organic matter suits it best. Propagation is by divison, layers, seeds, and cuttings made from the ripe wood and rooted under glass. The variety *C. nana* is a dwarf form about one foot high; it is well suited to the rockery.

Daphne Cneorum (see page 173).

Elaeagnus Pungens, Zone VII, Oleaster, is a stiff, spreading shrub that usually grows five or six feet high, but sometimes reaches twelve to fifteen feet. It is especially at home in the South; in fact, if it is planted as far north as New York City, it should be given a sheltered spot. Its delightfully fragrant small flowers appear in the fall, and the fruit turns red in the spring. This shrub is not at all fastidious as to soil; it thrives in poor ground that is well drained, but it does demand a sunny location. The supply can be increased by cuttings of half-ripe or mature wood, and by seeds.

The rich green glossy leaves of *E. pungens* are silvery on the underside. It can be used for background planting, and it grows successfully in seashore gardens.

Erica (see page 177).

Euonymus, Spindle-tree, comprises a remarkably versatile group of plants, some of which develop a shrubby growth, the ability to climb, or to form a good ground cover; these widely diversified habits of growth are found in the individual plant of several varieties, and they can be turned to different uses by careful pruning. If a shrub is required, the plant is kept clipped down to the height the particular kind reaches in a bushy form, and side shoots are tipped back to make a more compact growth; if the plant is to be turned into a climber, some of the shoots are removed in order to direct the strength of the plant into fewer branches and encourage them to shoot upwards into a vine. For a ground cover, *Euony-*

The tall **Chinese Fir** is an example of incorrect planting. It cuts off light and air from the windows, and obstructs the vista. This illustrates the necessity of selecting plants of the proper height for a given place. *Photographer, Caryl R. Firth.*

mus is allowed to grow in a natural way with a little clipping here and there.

Euonymus falls into two main groups: the evergreens and semi-evergreens, and the deciduous kinds. The splendid foliage and colorful fruits of many types have made it extremely valuable landscape material in its various adaptations. It is propagated by seeds, cuttings, and layers. The seeds are stratified and are sown the next spring; the cuttings are made in autumn from ripened wood.

Euonymus is susceptible to some of the ills that plants fall heir to, the most troublesome being scale. This is combatted by spraying with miscible oil early in the spring. In summer, when the young scales hatch, another spraying should be applied, using white oil emulsion that contains some nicotine sulphate. One word of caution, however; if the temperature is close to 90 degrees, this spray should not be used.

Euonymus is not exacting as to soil requirements, although a fertile soil is usually more acceptable; it will thrive in any good garden loam provided it is well drained.

E. patens, Zone VI, is a semi-evergreen variety. Its fine foliage usually remains on the plant throughout the winter months unless severe frost occurs, and new leaves appear quickly after the old ones have gone. It produces a generous number of very effective pinkish berries with seeds that are orange covered. In sun or shade this shrub will flourish; it can withstand the cold temperatures of New York, and if given a sheltered nook, it will grow successfully as far north as Massachusetts. This variety attains a height of about six to eight feet and develops into a compact bush. Sometimes procumbent branches strike root. If kept well pruned, it can be used as a hedge, and in the shrubbery border it provides an attractive foliage plant and adds color when in fruit.

E. Fortunei, Zone V, is the new name for *E. radicans.* A trailing evergreen, it will reach a height of about twenty feet when it can cling to a support with a rough surface. It has several varieties, and their characteristics qualify them to be put to various uses in the planting scheme.

E. Fortunei var. Carrierei grows a foot or more in height, and where a low evergreen hedge is needed it will answer the purpose admirably. It also makes a good climber, although in this capacity it is not as ambitious a grower as *E. Fortunei,* nor is it quite as hardy as *E. Fortunei* and the variety vegeta. It is not fastidious as to exposure and will grow well in

The corners of the house are softened with tall-growing shrubs. Compact Yews accent each side of the front door. *Photographer, H. Armstrong Roberts.*

sun or shade. The plants can be increased from seed that is stratified and sown in spring, from layers, or from cuttings made in July or August.

E. Fortunei var. colorata is a rapidly spreading evergreen that turns a brilliant crimson in the fall, and in the cold winter months it takes on a bronze color. This variety likes to grow in the full sunshine, where it attains a height of two feet. Along a low wall or as a ground cover it adds interest to the planting. It is propagated by stratifying the seed until the Spring, by layering, and by cuttings that are made in July or August.

E. Fortunei var. kewensis thrives in the shade or in the sun, but prefers partial shade. It grows two feet high in a good garden loam; however, it particularly likes soil that has been enriched with fertilizer. Where a small-leaved evergreen bank cover is required, *E. kewensis* will prove an excellent choice; in a rockery it provides a contrasting note in form and texture. It is also used as a climber.

E. Fortunei var. minima closely resembles *E. kewensis*. It reaches a height of three feet, which makes it good evergreen hedge material; in a rock garden it is used as an accent plant. As a climber and as a bank cover its small dark evergreen leaves are always an addition. It adapts itself to sunny or shady situations.

E. Fortunei var. radicans makes a good evergreen hedge three to four feet high, and it will grow happily in a sunny or shady location in any good soil; however, it prefers ground that is very fertile.

E. Fortunei var. vegeta is a low bush attaining a height of approximately four or five feet, which makes it useful as an evergreen hedge; it is also a vigorous climber, or it can be allowed to trail on the ground. It is very hardy and has splendid foliage, and when the orange-red berries are in fruit, it gives an exceptionally striking effect. It should be planted in a sunny exposure.

E. radicans acuta, Zone V, has glossy, pointed leaves that make it attractive where a low grower is needed—along a low wall, for instance. It grows to two and a half feet; as an evergreen ground cover it is also valuable. This variety prefers light shade.

E. japonica, Zone VII, is an upright-growing evergreen, but it is not hardy north of Philadelphia unless it is planted in a protected location. There are a number of varieties, some of which produce variegated leaves. It needs a sunny exposure and will tolerate cold temperatures better if given a sandy, well-drained soil. This plant is grown from hardwood cuttings. E. japonica grows eight to ten feet high and sometimes taller. It is well adapted for use as a hedge or as a specimen. For screening purposes it again proves its value; its dark-green, shiny leaves are always ornamental. It is one of the plants that will thrive at the seashore. The variety *E. japonica microphylla,* Boxleaf Burning-bush, produces small leaves, and it makes an attractive hedge in the warmer sections of the country (in the South and California).

Chapter VII

Evergreens — F through P

Ilex, Holly, in its many varieties is unquestionably one of the finest and most useful groups of evergreens in cultivation. There are species which fit into the smallest places as well as into the more spacious ones; these vary from the well-known American and English Hollies which grow into handsome trees laden with red berries, to the Chinese, and Japanese Holly, *Ilex crenata,* and its many lower growing compact varieties.

Hollies can be allowed to retain their natural height, or they can be sheared and kept down as low as from two to twelve feet, depending upon the species. Their uses are legion; wherever they are included they are always a welcome addition to the planting scheme, and throughout the year they rank high in ornamental value. As hedges and for foundation plantings they are excellent; the dwarf varieties are splendid for bordering terraces, patios, and walks. The bush forms are charming for softening walls, and as background plantings to set off any feature such as a pool or a flower border. Planted outside a picture window, a nearby specimen of American or English Holly covered with berries will bring a ray of winter cheer into the house. Owners of ranch-type and split-level homes who are looking for low-growing evergreens to plant under windows that are close to the ground will find the dwarf forms of *Ilex crenata* a real bonanza.

91

Holly can be planted in the full sun or in partial shade; in climates where the summers are excessively hot, locations that will give some protection from the sun are preferable. It flourishes in light, moist, but well-drained soil rich in humus; and as with most broad-leaved evergreens, a mulch of peat moss or hardwood sawdust that is well decomposed will protect its shallow root system and help keep the soil cool and moist.

The best planting season is in the spring just as growth starts, or in late August before the fall growth commences, so that the plants will become established before winter. Large specimens are a little difficult to move, but a good-sized ball of earth will keep the roots intact and reduce to a minimum the setback of transplanting. Unlike the majority of evergreens, Hollies do best when they are transplanted the same depth that they stood before; this is an important cultural point to observe, because deep planting all too often results in failure. After planting, a thorough watering should be given; subsequent watering should depend upon weather and soil conditions, some soils being less retentive of moisture than others. Too much moisture before the plants take hold of the soil will cause the roots to rot. Hollies grown for their decorative berries are pruned during the Christmas season; later trimming is done in the spring merely to increase the compactness and form of the plant.

Hollies are dioecious, which means that the plants are either male or female; and in order to ensure a good crop of berries, both sexes must be planted for pollination purposes. Since the male plant produces no berries, it can be planted in an inconspicuous spot. A larger crop of berries will be produced if the male plant is not too far away from the female plants; however, pollination has been known to take place when the male and female plants were half a mile from each other. One male specimen should pollinate twenty-five females, provided it is the same species as the female—the blooming period of the different kinds varies somewhat. Nurserymen are simplifying the problem of pollination by planting the two sexes together so that they will eventually form one plant. Other growers are grafting a male branch onto a female tree. Either method is satisfactory and is a decided asset to the small home owner who has space for only one bush or tree. The quantity of berries produced may vary from year to year according to the weather conditions that prevail at the time of bloom. In cloudy wet weather the bees that are busy pollinators are not so active; consequently the pollination necessary for the production of berries will be inadequate.

The Holly expert Mr. H. Gleason Mattoon finds that female Hollies will set berries without a male plant if they are sprayed with the weed-killer 2-4-D, which is actually a hormone. Four drops (dropped from a medicine dropper) of this chemical are used to one quart of water. Mr. Mattoon emphasizes the importance of following these proportions with the utmost care; too strong a solution will kill the trees. Use this spray when the blossoms first appear, and repeat it in three days. All the flowers do not open at the same time, and for this reason the second spray is required to catch the late-comers.

Hollies can be increased by cuttings taken in August or September after the new growth has hardened. The slips are rooted in a frame or under glass. Raising them from seed is a slow process; stratification is required, and germination does not usually occur before the second year. After they have sprouted, the seedlings can be grown in pots, and they make an unusual and attractive contribution to the house plants. In this way they are nursed through their infancy, and outdoor planting is deferred until they are large enough to stand the uncertainties of the weather. Red mites are apt to discolor the Holly leaves, but Malathion has proved to be efficacious in controlling this pest.

Home owners who would like to grow Hollies that are not particularly hardy in their locality can experiment by selecting the hardiest strains of the desired species. It is wise to purchase plants locally; these have had a chance to become acclimated and are more likely to succeed than if bought from a nursery in a different part of the country.

I. Aquifolium, Zone VI, English Holly, is highly prized for its glossy, rich-green foliage and showy red berries; it is an outstanding species. In common with the American Holly it attains a height of about thirty feet, and it is excellent for specimen plantings or for hedges. There is evidence that the hardier strains now being developed will make it possible to grow this species in sections of northern New York and Massachusetts. It is most important to select the hardiest varieties available in your locality. Another factor which enters into the growing of *I. Aquifolium* farther north is the change toward generally warmer temperatures on the continent of North America. From Philadelphia southward all strains will thrive; however, in the South a partly shady location should be chosen.

This planting was made one month after construction was completed.
Photographer, Emily Mayer.

I. centrochinensis (I. ciliospinosa, Zone VII?) is a hardy, small-leaved tree which grows to twenty feet; the leaves are not glossy, but its habit is dense, upright, and very ornamental. The male plant is laden with blossoms which makes it extremely showy when in bloom.

I. cornuta, Zone VII, Chinese Holly, is a shrub that grows about ten feet high. Its glossy foliage and bright red berries make it a favorite for growing in the warmer parts of the country.

I. cornuta Burfordii, Burford Holly, is a beautiful bushy shrub that grows to about ten feet. Its wax-like leaves and red berries are unusually attractive. For the small garden it is ideal, one of its valuable character-

The same planting seven years later. The shrubs each side of the front door are *Ilex crenata microphylla*. Photographer, *Bill Harris*.

istics being its ability to produce berries without a male plant. When the bushes are in bloom, syringe the flowers with a fine mist of water. If this is done, practically every blossom will set berries.

I. crenata, Zone VI, Japanese Holly, is a shrub from five to ten feet high and sometimes reaches a height of twenty feet. Its dark-green leaves and attractive habit of growth make it exceptionally decorative. It grows well in the Philadelphia area and is hardy as far north as Boston. Garden makers in the Mid-west will do well to plant *I. crenata rotundifolia* because of its ability to stand the hot sun. Some of the dwarf varieties well adapted for use wherever low evergreens are called for include: *Helleri* (one to one-and-a-half feet high), *Stokesi, Green Cushion,* and *Green Island.* The latter may grow a little higher than the others mentioned, but its habit of growth is more graceful and it can be kept pruned to the desired height. Other dwarf varieties are *nummularia, Kingsville,* and *microphylla,* Zone (V), Littleleaf Japanese Holly.

I. crenata convexa, Zone V, (*I. crenata bullata*), Convex-leaved Japanese Holly, can be planted in all but the coldest sections of this country; its close resemblance to Box makes it an ideal substitute for northern gardeners. It can grow into a shrub six to eight feet high and several feet in width, but unless conditions are very favorable its normal height is three to four feet. It grows slowly, lends itself admirably to trimming, and is one of the loveliest of all hedge plants. The new variety *Ilex convexa hetzi* seems destined to become a universal favorite; it grows faster, the leaves are slightly larger, and it is just as hardy as the *I. convexa.*

I. glabra, Zone III, Inkberry, is a light, graceful shrub that grows to six or eight feet; it has small leaves and black berries which add to its winter effect. This is a hardy bush which is useful for planting in shady places; it combines well with material that is heavier in its habit of growth, such as Rhododendrons.

I. opaca, Zone V, American Holly, grows into a handsome tree thirty to fifty feet in height. It can be used for a specimen or for a hedge; when used for the latter purpose, the annual trimming required to keep it within bounds increases its density, and it eventually develops into a beautiful hedge covered with red berries. The variety *Xanthocarpa* is a yellow-fruited form. Plants set four to six feet apart for a hedge will have a better chance to branch out into well-formed plants than those that are placed too close to each other; the latter are apt to become lanky. In its native habitat, American Holly ranges from Massachusetts to Florida and west to Texas and Missouri. There are various strains of this species that are superior to the type, and these improved, hardier varieties have increased the usefulness of the plant, making its cultivation possible in all parts of the country with the exception of some of the north-central states.

I. pedunculosa, Zone (V), Long-stalk Holly, is an outstanding broad-leaved evergreen for northern climates. It grows fifteen to twenty feet in height. This species, which is indigenous to China, does not resemble a Holly—in fact, it looks like a pear tree. The red berries are large and are

The spreading branches of American Holly give interest to the winter picture. *Photographer, the Roches.*

borne either singly or in groups of two or three on single stems. In appearance the fruit is similar to Montmorency cherries. Another useful Holly that appears to thrive in northern localities is *I. yunnanensis,* Zone VII?, Chinese Yunnan.

I. Pernyi, Zone VI, also a native of China, is a distinctive plant because of its diminutive leaves and compact, pyramidal shape; eventually it reaches a height of twenty feet. This type will produce berries without a male plant, especially if its flowers are syringed with a fine mist of water; however, the crop of berries will be more prolific if a male plant is included.

Juniperus.   Juniper, offers good dwarf forms for covering banks, for use in rock gardens, or wherever a low-growing evergreen is required.

Junipers will not tolerate shade. They thrive in open windswept locations that are sunny and dry. They can be raised in almost any soil, but show decided preference for ground that is sandy or even gravelly. Keep the earth around the plants well cultivated so that it will not cake. Prune in the spring when the young growth is on the plants. Very little trimming will be needed; however, they can be kept sheared if a formal effect is desired. During the summer any straggly shoots that develop can be tipped back from time to time.

Junipers are alternate hosts for apple rust; consequently they should be planted several hundred feet away from apple trees. If given a northeastern exposure, their foliage will be much less apt to discolor during the winter months.

Junipers can be propagated by seeds that are stratified for one year, after which time they are sown; however, germination will not take place for two or three years. They can also be increased by cuttings made in August; these slips are planted in a cold frame and should be kept shaded and watered until the roots develop. Insert the cuttings in a layer of sand placed over the soil and give ample winter protection to the frame.

J. chinensis Sargenti, J. horizontalis var. Bar Harbor, J. procumbens; and *Douglasii,* are all included among the best dwarf forms.

J. chinensis Pfitzeriana, is a spreading, feathery shrub which sometimes reaches a height of eight feet. It is very popular and is used extensively for foundation and entrance plantings, as well as for accent purposes. In winter, breakage is likely to occur unless the snow is kept brushed off the branches. It is a good plant for seashore gardens.

The rich green of the Yews provides strong contrast to the lighter shade of the Junipers. *Photographer, Paul E. Genereux.*

Laurel is at home in both naturalistic and formal settings. *Photographer, the Roches.*

Kalmia Latifolia, Zone IV or (III), Mountain-Laurel, is known by all garden lovers for its beauty. Its showy flowers range in color from white to pale pink and rose pink. It is one of the favorites of all broad-leaved evergreens. A native of North America, it abounds naturally in wooded and mountain areas in the eastern part of the country. It grows from five to ten feet, and under especially favorable conditions it attains a much greater height.

Laurel belongs to the same family as Rhododendrons and Azaleas (Ericaceae) and in common with them requires an acid soil which contains an ample supply of organic matter. It will grow in dense shade but much prefers partial shade. For profusion of bloom, sun is required; in fact, Laurel will grow well in the full sun provided it is kept adequately mulched.

This shrub is splendid for foundation plantings, groupings on banks, as under-planting, and as facers to Rhododendrons and other taller growing bushes. It is ideal for naturalistic gardens and is extremely showy when planted in masses.

A plant that has lost its lower leaves can be rejuvenated by being cut back to within a few inches of the ground in the early spring; this will stimulate the growth of young shoots from the ground up. Feeding with an acid fertilizer, and mulching will also encourage the new growth.

Leaf spot and blight sometimes attack Laurel; these diseases can be handled with sprayings of Ferbam applied at ten-day intervals. All affected leaves should be picked from the ground as well as from the bush and burned.

Laurel is propagated by seeds, cuttings, and layers; however, it is always a slow process.

Kalmia angustifolia, Zone II, Sheep-Laurel, (Lamb-kill), is so called because its leaves are thought to be poisonous to sheep. As a matter of fact, there is more to support the theory that the foliage of Mountain-Laurel is poisonous to sheep, calves, and goats. Sheep-Laurel is a hardy shrub. It grows three feet tall and bears purple or crimson flowers; the foliage is light green in color. It is less ornamental than Mountain-Laurel, but it fits in well for naturalistic plantings, as a facer, or for mass effect.

Ledum in its native habitat is found growing in swampy land and damp wooded areas; it is indigenous to the colder regions of North America. Its hardiness and its evergreen foliage make this plant useful for naturalizing where congenial soil requirements exist; it grows to three feet in height. The leaves of the species *L. groenlandicum,* Zone II, Labrador Tea, are thought to have been used in the North as a substitute for tea during the days of the War of Independence.

Ledum does well in sun or partial shade, and prefers moist, light, woodsy soil. Its white flowers appear in early summer, and its attractive narrow leaves are fragrant when crushed. Propagation is by seeds, layers and division. *L. glandulosum,* Zone V or VI?, is a very attractive, graceful shrub.

Leucothoe Catesbaei, Zone IV, Drooping Leucothoe, is a lovely low-growing shrub which bears clusters of white bell-shaped flowers along the stems in early spring. It does not often grow over three feet high, and it has a graceful, open habit of growth. It combines splendidly with Rhododendrons, Laurels and Azaleas, and is extremely decorative for use as a facer or as a filler between the larger growing evergreens. Being a low grower it is qualified for planting under windows. It does not form a sufficiently compact bush to make it desirable for use as a specimen. Leucothoe will stand dense shade, but partial shade is preferable. It likes a well-drained, light, peaty soil in situations that are protected from high winds. The foliage has a tendency to take on bronzy or purplish tints during the winter; this discoloration can be lessened if the shrubs are planted where they have winter shade, particularly during February and March. If the plants require renovation or if they winter-kill, they can be cut back close to the ground in the spring to encourage the growth of new shoots which will re-clothe the plant.

Leucothoe is propagated by seed, by division of underground runners, by cuttings, and by layers. Seeds are produced abundantly and are best sown under glass in bulb pans containing sand and sphagnum moss. The transplanted seedlings should be kept under glass until they are about six inches high.

Ligustrum, Privet, is most generally seen in one of its many deciduous species; however, evergreen kinds are extremely useful for home garden plantings. They are not reliably hardy as far north as Philadelphia, and when grown in that latitude the plants may winter-kill badly. In comman with the other Privets, growth is rapid, and with the arrival of spring, new shoots will soon replace the winter loss.

Privet is an adaptable plant and thrives under the adverse conditions of city yards, seashore, and windswept locations; it is drought-resistant and free from pests; furthermore, it will grow in practically any soil. The evergreen kinds will thrive in sun or shade. They make splendid hedges and are good for specimens; in fact, they are well suited to almost any type of home garden planting.

L. japonicum, Zone VII?, Japanese Privet, is a handsomer species than the *L. lucidum.* Its flowers appear in effective panicles, and the bush attains a height of ten feet. This species is not reliably hardy as far north as Philadelphia, but wherever it grows happily, it is a real contribution to the landscape effect. It is excellent for the small garden.

L. japonicum var. coriaceum (rotundifolium) has very dark, rich-green foliage which sets off the flowers to advantage. It is definitely a slow grower and eventually reaches a height of six feet.

L. japonicum var. ciliatum has soft-green, fleshy leaves. It develops into a shrub about six feet high.

L. japonicum Suwanee River is a hardier form which has recently been introduced; it is said to grow as far north as New York City.

The evergreen Privets are splendid for use as background plants, for giving seclusion, for foundations, and as specimens.

L. lucidum, Zone VII, Glossy Privet, grows into a handsome tree in warm climates where it reaches a height of twenty to thirty feet. The fragrant white flowers are of high ornamental value in the genial temperatures. Farther north, it remains shrubby and can be kept moderately low by pruning. The blooms are followed by blue-black berries. It is one of those plants that will solve the problem of shade, although it thrives better in a sunny situation.

L. sinense, Zone VII, Chinese Privet, is suitable for hedges and for specimens in mild climates. It is an upright-growing, compact, shapely shrub. In colder climates the foliage is apt to burn in winter and sometimes falls. This bush becomes twelve or more feet high.

An annual pruning helps to keep the shrubs mentioned above shapely and compact; this is usually done in spring. Sometimes repeated trimmings are required to keep the plant bushy.

Lonicera, Honeysuckle, is usually seen in one of the deciduous forms; however, *L. nitida* and *L. pileata* are worth-while additions to the evergreen planting. (For growing requirements, see page 199.)

Osmanthus gives a welcome touch of green to the winter scene. *Photographer, the Roches.*

L. nitida, Zone VII, Box Honeysuckle, is a shrub of great value, and it is evergreen in mild climates. Unfortunately, it is not hardy north of Delaware, although it is grown in protected locations in the Philadelphia area where it is used for foundations and specimens. In the South it becomes a very beautiful shrub, and in addition to its other uses it is an attractive plant for hedge work. Under congenial conditions it grows about six feet high. The fragrant white flowers are followed by blue-purple berries. This bush will also thrive at the seashore.

L. pileata, Zone (V), Privet Honeysuckle, is a shrub four feet tall which comes to our gardens from China. It is a most desirable shrub for foundation plantings and is hardier than *L. nitida;* however, in colder climates it becomes semi-evergreen. It will tolerate light shade. The fragrant white flowers appear in May; the violet-purple berries contribute to the fall color.

Mahonia Aquifolium, Zone V, Oregon Holly-Grape, is a striking shrub with glossy leaves which resemble the foliage of Holly. It usually does not grow more than three feet high, but sometimes it reaches six feet. The effective spikes of bright yellow flowers appear in April or May; these are followed by clusters of blue-black berries with a blue or violet "bloom." *Mahonia Aquifolium* is quite hardy and will endure a temperature of 5 or 10 degrees below zero, provided these temperatures are not of long duration.

One of the chief assets of *Mahonia* is its adaptability to a wide range of soils. It likes a moist soil but will grow in poor land and in ground that is heavy, sandy, or even gravelly. In the North it is best to plant *Mahonia* where it will be protected from strong winds. For best winter effect a northeastern exposure is preferable, because the foliage will be less apt to scorch if it is shielded from the winter sun. *Mahonia* will grow in the shade, but it prefers a location that is only partly shady.

An annual spring pruning wil lhelp to keep the shrub low and shapely. It is not inclined to branch freely, but it spreads by means of runners or low branches that strike root. An occasional fertilizing with bone meal or well-rotted manure will stimulate growth.

Mahonia is frequently used as an under-planting to trees; in combination with other evergreens its distinctive foliage gives a contrasting note. Its habit of growth is not sufficiently symmetrical to qualify it for use as a specimen.

Pieris japonica provides an attractive background of luxuriant green for this small garden pool. *Owner, Mrs. Frances V. Finletter, L. A. Courtesy Horticulture. Photographer, the Roches.*

This shrub is propagated by seeds sown when ripe; they are stratified in the fall and sown the following spring. Plants can also be raised from suckers, layers, and cuttings of the half-ripe wood rooted under glass.

M. nervosa, Zone V, Cascades Mahonia, is a hardy, shrubby ground cover that is excellent for shady places. It grows about one or two feet tall and spreads by means of suckers. The purple fruit ripens in August.

M. repens, Zone V, is a hardy, low-growing form that is useful as a ground cover; it grows ten or twelve inches high and spreads liberally by means of suckers.

Osmanthus, Holly Olive, belongs to the Olive Family; it is hardy as far north as Philadelphia, provided it is given a sheltered location. Most soils of average fertility will meet its growing needs, if enough organic matter, such as peat moss, is worked into the ground to supply acidity. *Osmanthus* can be planted in the sun or partial shade. It is propagated from cuttings of half-ripened wood which are grown under glass.

O. Fortunei grows to six feet and works well into the planting scheme. Espaliered against the wall, it provides an attractive feature, and in northern climates the warmth of a house wall gives welcome protection.

O. ilicifolius, (O. Aquifolium) Zone VI, is extremely desirable for specimen planting where it has ample space to develop into a very handsome shrub. It grows seven to twenty feet tall. It is equally good for hedges, background plantings, and softening the corners of the house. The fragrant blooms are followed by blue-black berries.

Pieris, the floribunda and japonica species, are among the finest of all broad-leaved evergreens. Their handsome foliage and attractive stocky growth make them valuable for many uses, such as foundation plantings, specimens, entrance plantings, facers and fillers in combination with other evergreens, and wall softeners. Planted back of a pool or any other garden feature, they set it off superbly. *Pieris* will grow in sun or shade, in ground that is light and moist. An acid soil is a requisite; therefore an ample amount of peat moss or of leaf mold should be worked into the earth.

The plants can be increased by cuttings made in August from side shoots; these should root in two and a half months. Keep the cuttings in a propagating kit with a plastic cover, or under a glass jar. The young plants must be wintered in the house. Pieris can also be propagated by air-layering.

Pieris floribunda, Zone IV, Mountain Andromeda, the native Andromeda, is a happy solution for shady situations, and it is easy to grow when
it is once established. It is hardy as far north as Massachusetts. This
round-topped shrub eventually reaches six feet in height, and is spreading
in its habit of growth. It has the decided asset of being free from pests;
however, in the last few years a blight has attacked it in some sections
of the country, and for this reason the variety japonica has become more
commonly used. Although this species is native to the high altitude of
the southern Appalachian Mountains, it is not often found as a wild plant.
In England it has been cultivated in gardens for over a century.

P. japonica, Zone (V), Japanese Pieris, is a more decorative species
than the native one, but it is not as hardy as *P. floribunda,* and in the
North the flower buds are susceptible to winter injury. It will grow in
sheltered locations as far north as Philadelphia, but on Long Island it is
not reliably hardy. It will tolerate temperatures of zero or slightly lower.
The foliage is glossy, and the pendulous white flower clusters which
appear in April are real harbingers of spring. *P. japonica* can be grown
in the shade, but a sunny exposure is necessary for abundant bloom.
It reaches a height of approximately five feet but can be kept low with
pruning. *P. japonica var. pygmaea* is a dwarf kind that is suitable for
use where a lower-growing shrub is required.

Prunus Laurocerasus, Zone VI-VII, Cherry-Laurel, develops into a
beautiful specimen in the South and on the Pacific Coast where it grows
luxuriantly. As hedge material and for background and foundation planting it again proves its value. Cherry-Laurel grows best in a rich soil and
prefers a protected location; it sometimes attains a height of twenty-five
feet. Its glossy, dark-green leaves and attractive appearance make it a
splendid subject for home garden planting. It has the important advantage of being remarkably free from diseases. In southern climates, Cherry
Laurel should be given a shady place in which to grow. Propagation is by
layers and by long cuttings taken in summer when the wood has ripened.

There are various forms of this shrub which differ in hardiness, habit
of growth, and height. Some types are hardy as far north as Washington,
D. C. The variety *Schipkaensis* can be grown as far north as central
New York.

Pyracantha, Firethorn, with its showy berries is one of the most outstanding of all berried plants. It lends itself admirably to various uses;

Before the planting was made.

This "after" picture shows what imagination and good planning can accomplish. The charming terrace took form after the fence was erected, largely concealing the adjacent garage. The *Pyracantha* has been espaliered on the fence in an informal pattern. *Owners, Mr. and Mrs. Wyllys P. Ames. Photographer, the Roches.*

a well-grown specimen ablaze with its red or orange-red berries is a sight rarely surpassed. Espaliered against a wall it provides a distinctive feature, and as a hedge or planted along a fence line. *Pyracantha* contributes a full measure of color to the fall and winter effect. It is also excellent for softening the corners of the house and to clothe a broad expanse of wall.

Pyracantha will grow in partial shade, but for a generous production of berries, full sun is required. Almost any well-drained garden soil will meet its needs, but slightly alkaline ground is preferable; if the soil is naturally acid, the addition of a little limestone is beneficial. *Pyracantha* is difficult to transplant, and large plants should be moved with generous balls of earth. It is best to purchase pot plants because these are easier to establish. The proper season for setting out the plants is in the spring. This shrub does not usually exceed six feet, but occasionally it develops into a bush twenty feet in height.

Pyracantha can be shaped to the desired form by pruning or shearing. If the tops of the branches are kept tipped back, a dense growth will be encouraged. Spring is the usual time for pruning; however, if this is done before the flowers appear, many potential berries will be sacrificed. If pruning is attended to during the blooming period, it may then be possible to limit the cuttings to non-flowering shoots. Of course, some of the fruit may have to be sacrificed for the future shapeliness of the shrub.

Propagation is by seeds, layers, and cuttings. Slips are taken in July and are rooted in a frame or in boxes containing a layer of sand three or four inches deep. The container is covered with glass and placed in a shady spot.

Pyracantha coccinea, Zone VI, and its variety *P. coccinea Lalandii* are the hardiest forms and can be grown in protected places as far north as New York, although in that latitude they are not reliably hardy. The *Lalandii* variety is the hardiest one, and its large showy orange-red berries are finer than the red fruits of the *coccinea.*

Other desirable species suitable for mild climates are *angustifolia,* Zone VII; *crenulata,* Zone VII?; and *Gibbsii,* Zone VI?. All of these types bear red berries.

P. crenulata var. flava, produces yellow fruit.

yracantha espaliered in a formal design. *Photographer, the Roches.*

Chapter VIII

Evergreens—Q through Z

Rhododendrons and **Azaleas** belong to the Ericaceae Family, *Azaleas* forming a "Series" in the *Rhododendron* genus. Their growing requirements are similar. The evergreen types of *Azaleas* are discussed at the end of the *Rhododendron* culture. (For deciduous *Azaleas* see page 146.)

The ornamental value of *Rhododendrons* ranks high among the broad-leaved evergreens. The decorative flowers of many of the species and the handsome foliage of both hybrids and natives make them among the most popular of all woody ornamentals. Their uses in designing the home grounds are numerous. *Rhododendrons* are ideal for foundation and entrance plantings, as well as along boundaries where they provide privacy from the neighbors; for naturalistic groupings in wooded lots and to soften a long line of wall, they are enjoyed throughout the year. Many of the hybrids are lovely when used as specimens. *Rhododendrons* are excellent in providing seclusion for outdoor living areas. In combination with other evergreens and deciduous material, they give a rich contrast in foliage, form, and texture.

Rhododendrons are easy to grow. Select a suitable location, give them the kind of soil they crave, and keep the ground around the plants well mulched. If these cultural points are observed, the planting will take care of itself with little upkeep.

113

A charming living area has been developed in a naturalistic setting. *Rhododendron* and Laurel are used as facers to the trees, and as a border to the paved area. *Photographer, Paul E. Genereux.*

Rhododendrons prefer partial shade and definitely dislike hot, dry situations, such as exist against walls with a southern exposure which reflect the intensity of the summer's sun. When they are planted in the full sun, watering, fertilizing, and mulching must be given to compensate for the lack of shade and moisture which they enjoy. In complete shade, *Rhododendrons* can be used to supply greens; however, little or no bloom can be expected unless the plants receive one or two hours of sun a day.

Protection from high winds is another essential. In neighborhoods where houses are built close to each other, this does not usually present a problem; however, on properties that are open and windswept a windbreak will be needed. A planting of shrubbery or trees so placed as to break the force of the prevailing winds will answer the purpose.

The feeding roots of *Rhododendrons* grow close to the surface of the ground; therefore if they are to be planted under trees, it is wiser to select trees that have roots that forage deep into the ground for their food and water supply, so that their roots will not compete seriously with those of the *Rhododendrons*. For this reason, conifers such as Hemlocks, Pines, Spruces, and Firs make good companions for them. Oak trees are also acceptable; furthermore their leaves liberate much needed acidity in the process of decomposition. If possible, don't plant them under Maples, Elms, Willows, Poplars, Birches, or Cherries. These trees have surface-feeding roots and their foliage becomes alkaline as decomposition progresses. Of course, this does not mean that *Rhododendrons* cannot be successfully grown under trees that possess surface-feeding root systems, but in such instances the plants must be kept adequately watered, fertilized, and mulched.

Rhododendrons do not thrive in the arid sections of the country. In regions where the soil is naturally alkaline, it must be kept constantly acidified to enable them to grow satisfactorily.

In woodsy situations where soil conditions are naturally enriched with leaf mold, no special preparation will be required. When this is not the case, the ground should be especially prepared by excavating the hole to a depth of eighteen inches and filling it with soil consisting of 50 percent leaf mold or peat moss and 50 percent garden soil. A light, well-drained, spongy soil is much to be preferred to one that is heavy; however, if the latter is the only kind available, its texture can be improved by incorporating into it plenty of organic matter and sand.

Rhododendrons demand an acid soil which has an acid content ranging between pH 4.5 and pH 5.2. In alkaline ground the plants become yellow and sickly; and if this condition is not corrected, the bushes will eventually die. A foliar spray of chelated iron combined with an application of a soil acidifier should remedy the trouble. One pound of Sulphur to each one hundred square feet of soil, together with a good supply of organic matter, will increase the acid content.

Rhododendrons can be planted almost any time of the year by an experienced nurseryman, but the amateur will do well to restrict his planting to the fall or the spring. In the North, spring planting is preferable, because the shrubs will have the benefit of the growing season in which to become established before the winter sets in. At whatever time the planting is done, the shrubs should be lifted with good balls of earth; this will keep the roots intact and reduce the setback of transplanting to a minimum. Make the planting hole larger than the ball of earth to facilitate firming the soil around the ball. Set the plants slightly deeper than they stood before, and work a generous amount of peat moss around the balled roots before closing the hole. Water both the ground and the leaves thoroughly and mulch the planting with oak leaves or peat moss; this covering should be kept on the ground throughout the year. In cold climates a mulch of oak leaves six or eight inches thick, spread in the fall, is none too much for protection through the winter months. In the spring this mulch will have settled considerably, and if it is deeper than two or three inches, remove the surplus, which will leave an adequate covering for the growing season; the following fall a fresh supply of leaves will be in order.

Rhododendrons should never be cultivated. Any weeds that appear must be pulled by hand; otherwise the surface roots will be disturbed. Immediately after the blooming period, remove the faded blooms to conserve the strength of the plants for the production of next year's flower buds; this is an important detail in rhododendron culture and one which is usually overlooked. In dry spells, both the ground and the topgrowth should be well watered; in fact, *Rhododendrons* should never be allowed to dry out. Always water the foliage as well as the roots.

As with most plants, feeding helps to maintain a vigorous growth. In the North no fertilizer should be given later than June first, since growth ceases in July. Later feeding will only encourage new shoots that will not

The asymmetrical effect of the *Rhododendrons* on one side of the steps and the Pine tree on the other gives informality and contrast. *Photographer, Paul E. Genereux.*

have time to harden before frost overtakes them. Cottonseed Meal, or one of the fertilizers on the market especially prepared for Rhododendrons and Azaleas, can be used. Some growers recommend a mixture of two parts superphosphate to one part potassium nitrate; about a trowelful of this combination is spread evenly around a shrub measuring approximately three feet high.

Rhododendrons are propagated by seeds, cuttings, and layers. The large flowering varieties are usually increased by grafting—a highly specialized job best done by professionals. Seeds are gathered when they are ripe and are sown thinly in pots filled with peat moss or sphagnum moss. They are sown in the winter, kept in the house, and covered with plastic or with a pane of glass. They should never be watered with a strong spray; a gentle sprinkling is definitely necessary in order not to dislodge the seed. When germination takes place, the covering is removed and the seedlings are kept in an airy, light room. When they are large enough to transplant, shift them into pots containing a mixture of peat moss, sand, and soil. Cuttings root slowly and are difficult for the inexperienced gardener to handle; they are made during the summer or fall and planted in a shaded frame, or preferably in a greenhouse where bottom heat can be supplied. A simpler method of propagation to follow is by means of layers (see pages 41–46).

To combat mildew, use a Sulphur spray in the proportions of three level tablespoons of Wettable Sulphur to one gallon of water. Die-back of the shoots is treated by removing the affected parts and spraying the bush with Bordeaux. If spots develop on the leaves and stems, spray repeatedly with Ferbam. Weevils that eat holes on the margins of the leaves are controlled with Chlordane dusted on the soil and branches. Lace bugs are especially troublesome on *Rhododendrons* grown in the sun; they feed on the under-surfaces of the leaves, extracting the sap and discoloring the foliage. They can be eliminated by sprayings with Malathion applied during the last week of May and again ten days later. If a later brood appears, repeated spraying will be required. A root fungus sometimes causes wilt, and branches or whole plants may be destroyed during the summer. Replant in fresh ground that is well supplied with organic matter to increase acidity. No spray or dust should be used when the sun is shining on the shrubs or when the temperature is in the nineties.

The genus *Rhododendron* is comprised of about eight hundred species

The high-headed tree on the right allows adequate light for an under-planting of *Azaleas* to produce abundant bloom. *Courtesy Mahoney Construction Company. Photographer, Bill Harris.*

Foundation planting of *Azaleas. Photographer, J. Horace McFarland Company.*

and more than two thousand varieties. Many of the Hybrids are un-questionably the most desirable from the standpoint of bloom effect. The best course to pursue is to visit a nursery during the blooming period and to select the desired color. Sometimes the color descriptions are mis-leading. On this score it is well to bear in mind the fact that the exact shade of the same variety will differ slightly, depending upon soil and weather conditions. Different *Rhododendrons* eventually attain different heights, and some varieties tolerate deeper shade than others. These characteristics should be considered when you are purchasing the plants so that you will choose the right variety for the space allocated to them.

A few of the leading *Rhododendrons* among the many species in cultivation are the Catawba Hybrids, the Fortunei Hybrids, R. carolini-anum, and R. maximum.

Rhododendron carolinianum, Zone V, Carolina Rhododendron, is a hardy species. Ordinarily one of the lower-growing kinds, reaching ap-proximately four feet in height, it forms a compact shrub. This species does well in full sun or in partial shade. The flowers and leaves are smaller than those of the catawbiense, and it is available in pale pink, delicate rose pink, and white.

R. catawbiense, Zone IV, Catawba Hybrids, grow into large, handsome plants six to twelve feet in height. They, too, are compact in their habit of growth.

R. Fortunei Hybrids, Zone VI, succeed in mild climates south of Phila-delphia, but some can be grown as far north as New York. They come in an assortment of softer shades than those of the Catawba Hybrids, and they attain a height of approximately six to ten feet. Because of their superior shades, these and other hybrids should be used wherever climatic conditions permit.

R. maximum, Zone III, Rosebay Rhododendron, grows to twelve feet or higher; it is a native kind and an excellent species for naturalistic planting. It is hardy, but not nearly as effective in bloom as the hybrids.

Evergreen Azaleas.   The culture of *Azaleas* differs from that of "true" *Rhododendrons* in three respects: *Azaleas* stand more sun, they are slightly more tolerant of an alkaline soil, and they can stand more wind than "true" Rhododendrons. Most *Azaleas* are deciduous (see page 146), but there are a few evergreen kinds that are extremely valuable to garden makers, though they are not as hardy as the deciduous kinds.

Most of the enemies of *Azaleas* are the same as those of *Rhododen-*

drons. Azaleas are particularly susceptible to leaf spot and blight. Spray every two weeks from early July to mid-August to combat leaf spot, using one and three-quarter level tablespoons of Perzate zineb fungicide per gallon of water. When blight appears, pick off and burn all affected parts; then spray with fixed copper containing 50 percent metallic copper, using two level tablespoons to one gallon of water. This should be applied after the blooming period.

Azalea amoena Zone (V), (Kurume), grows into an extremely handsome specimen. It is a pity that its magenta flowers preclude its general use. Planted by itself against a background of greens, the color of its blooms is more acceptable than when combined with any other color, and it is noteworthy for its splendid dense habit of growth. It is often used as a specimen.

Azalea Hinodegiri (Kurume), Zone VI-VII, is also a compact grower. Its flowers ar a brilliant rosy red and too strong a shade to combine with the pastels of other blooms. It appears at its best when planted in front of evergreens. Among the many desirable varieties in the Kurume group might be mentioned Pink Pearl and Coral Bells. Kurume Azaleas are not reliably hardy north of Philadelphia, and where the winters are very cold they are semi-evergreen and the foliage becomes discolored.

Azalea ledifolia alba, Zone (V), *A. mucronata, R. indicum,* Snow Azalea, is one of the finest Azaleas in cultivation. The large showy white flowers add greatly to the spring flower display at tulip time. It has an attractive rounded shape that is compact from the ground up, and its fine foliage gives a good effect at all seasons. It is unexcelled for foundation plantings, where it can be used as a facer for taller growing material; it is also used for accent and specimen purposes. It is hardy as far north as Long Island, and it is frequently grown farther north in protected locations. Varieties come in blush-pink, lilac, and mauve, but the white form is the finest.

Sarcococca Confusa, Sweet Box, develops into a compact shrub suitable for planting in mild climates. It grows about four feet high; the fragrant flowers are followed by black fruit. It requires a shady location, and can be grown in soils that are heavy. *S. ruscifolia,* Zone VII?, bears dark red fruit and grows to six feet. The white flowers are fragrant and the leaves are glossy. This species grows in both partial or dense shade.

Taxus, Yew, has rich green foliage that remains unchanged in color throughout the year. This quality is a real asset to the home owner who gardens for winter as well as for summer effect. Because of its dense and varied habit of growth, and its ability to stand severe pruning, the Yew is splendid for hedges, foundation plantings, topiary work, accent points, specimens, and the lower-growing forms are good for banks and for planting under windows. In fact the different varieties are used for every kind of ornamental home ground planting; actually they are more universally planted than any other evergreen. There is a Yew that will fit into every garden, whether it be a dwarf type one foot high, a taller shrub, or one that turns into a large tree.

Other factors that contribute to the popularity of Yews is their easy culture, and the fact that they are practically immune to insects and diseases. These plants are not at all difficult to transplant, they will grow

This entrance planting is unusually treated with the Yew hedge enclosure. Note the sharply broken lines of plant material which add interest. *Photographer, the Roches.*

A shady corner offers a splendid opportunity for providing an extra
nook for outdoor living. Evergreens soften the tall redwood fence line.
Neighboring trees give height and background to this charming, simple
feature. *Owner, Miss Gertrude Ely. Courtesy The American Home.
Photographer, the Roches.*

in sun or shade, and in any average garden loam, however, a moist soil enriched with organic matter is preferable.

The black vine weevil that attacks Laurel sometimes gives trouble. The larvae eat the roots and cause a yellowing of the foliage. It can be checked successfully with Chlordane dusted on the branches and on the surface of the soil around the bush.

A male plant should be included in the planting if berry production is an objective. There is a yellow-fruiting variety, but the majority of the Yews bear translucent red berries that are perishable and shrivel when frost overtakes them.

There are not many species of Yews, but there are a number of varieties, some of the outstanding of which are given below, together with a few suggestions for their uses.

Taxus baccata, Zone VI, English Yew, does not usually exceed fifteen feet in this country. It is not reliably hardy north of New Jersey. As specimens, for foundation plantings, or for hedges, it gives a rich effect.

T. baccata fastigiata, Irish Yew, is a distinctive columnar form, but it is not hardy north of Delaware. The variety *lutea* produces yellow fruit. Its rich, deep-green foliage makes it most desirable for hedge work, foundation and accent plantings. It gives a very handsome effect wherever used.

T. baccata repandens, Zone IV, is a decidedly hardier variety of this species. It is a lovely, dense, low-growing, spreading, graceful shrub which reaches a height of about three feet. It is excellent for foundation plantings or for accents on each side of the entrance to the property; it is one of the most useful varieties. The variety *aurea* is a very desirable "golden-leaved" form; another variety with variegated leaves is *Washingtoni.*

T. canadensis stricta, is splendid for low hedges and can be kept pruned to one to two feet. It prefers a northern exposure in a shady location.

T. cuspidata capitata eventually reaches twenty feet and is good for use as a specimen and for background planting.

T. cuspidata densa can be kept trimmed to one foot and is the densest of all Yews; it is suitable for low hedges and for rock gardens.

T. cuspidata nana is frequently called *brevifolia,* but this is a misnomer. It is a slow grower and well suited to small properties; it is very spreading and dense in its habit, attaining a height of two to three feet, and is thus a good plant for medium-sized hedges.

The evergreen *Viburnum rhytidophyllum*, Leather-leaf Viburnum, with its showy white flowers, handsome foliage and effective berries is a noteworthy shrub. *Photographer, the Roches.*

T. media Hatfieldi is a compact shrubby grower, excellent for hedges, foundation and background plantings.

T. media Hicksi is unsurpassed for hedges and for foundations; its columnar growth can be kept pruned to two to five feet in height.

T. Sieboldii, Zone IV, is a spreading, shrubby type, adapted to background plantings, specimens, or to soften the corners of the house.

Yews are propagated readily by cuttings taken from half-ripe or fully ripe wood rooted under glass. They are also increased by seeds.

Vaccinium Ovatum, Zone VII, Evergreen Blueberry, is a shrub eight to twelve feet tall which is highly valued for its handsome, glossy, rich-green leaves. It is native to the Pacific Coast and is planted extensively in the Pacific Northwest. It is not reliably hardy in the eastern part of the country. It is used extensively for greens in cut-flower arrangements, and whenever it is hardy it makes a splendid shrub in background plantings, as specimens, and for softening the corners of the house. It likes partial shade and an acid soil; this bush grows successfully at the seashore. In May it bears pink flowers, and later on it produces black berries. Evergreen Blueberry is a good shrub for all-year-round effect.

Viburnum in the evergreen species is not seen nearly as frequently as in the deciduous kinds which form the large majority. Their growing requirements are given in Chapter XV. The evergreen species are extremely valuable garden subjects, and in localities where they thrive they are always an addition to the garden composition. They are well suited for use as specimens, and in the background of the shrubbery border they provide substance; they are also splendid for giving seclusion and height wherever a tall-growing shrub is required.

V. rhytidophyllum, Zone (V), Leather-leaf Viburnum, is the only species that can be grown in the North. In protected situations it will stand zero temperatures; however, in extremely cold weather it is apt to die back. This shrub is not considered to be hardy north of Philadelphia. It is striking in appearance, with large crinkly leaves, and it grows approximately ten feet high. Its showy white blooms are followed by red berries which later change to black. In combination with other shrubs it provides a decidedly sharp contrast in texture and color of foliage.

V. tinus, Laurestinus, is the best of all the evergreen kinds. Unfortunately it is not hardy and thrives only in mild climates. It grows eight or ten feet high and develops into a stunning, compact specimen. Although it prefers a sunny exposure, it will stand the shade. It is subject to thrips and spider mites; however, its variety *lucidum* is free from pests and is a stronger grower with decorative lustrous leaves. It is the superior variety of the type and should be the one selected.

Pachysandra is one of the best evergreen ground covers, and it is easy to grow. *Photographer, the Roches.*

Chapter IX

Evergreen Ground Covers

Ground covers are among the indispensables in solving many garden problems. There are varieties that will fill the needs of different situations. In this valuable group of plants are types that like a sunny location, while others prefer shade or partial shade. Certain kinds grow best in rich soil; others will thrive on a crust in poor ground. Under the shade of trees and shrubs they are excellent, and in many would-be lawn areas where grass refuses to grow, ground covers clothe the otherwise bare earth with their luxuriant verdure; they are also an answer to the problem of holding the grade of banks.

Many a nook where planting space is restricted can be brought to life by using ground covers. For bordering terraces and for tucking into small beds on terraces or patios, they give a finishing touch. Under windows close to the ground where the plant material should be low at all times, neatly clipped beds of Periwinkle, Pachysandra, or Sarcococca fill the need. Ground covers are also useful for bordering a walk, for softening the pedestal of a statue, a bird bath, or a sun dial.

There are many plants adapted to ground cover uses; a few of the important evergreen kinds follow.

Arctostaphylos Uva-Ursi, Zone II, Bearberry, is a modest, charming ground cover with a formidable name for a plant that grows only a few inches high. It is a splendid hardy type that is indigenous to various parts of the Northern Hemisphere. The small vivid green leaves take on bronzy tints in the fall. Bearberry grows in sun or partial shade and fills the important need of thriving in ground that is too poor for most plants. It is excellent for covering sandy banks and for seashore and city yard plantings. Good drainage and acid soil is all it asks, and in ground not naturally acid peat moss or leaf mold will supply this requisite.

Propagation is no problem because the prostrate branches take root, and rooted clumps can be lifted ready to start life on their own. Plants found growing in their native haunts are difficult to transplant; it is wiser to purchase established stock from a nursery.

Cotoneaster Dammeri, Zone V?, is a hardy evergreen ground cover with trailing branches that take root and hold the soil. It grows one foot

Rhododendrons, Yews and English Ivy thrive in this city garden.
Photographer, Paul, E. Genereux.

tall; it likes the sun but will tolerate a little shade. The white flowers are not showy; these are followed by red fruit.

Euonymus in its various forms provides decorative ground covers with glossy, rich-green foliage. The E. Fortunei varieties kewensis, vegeta, minima, and colorata are suitable for this purpose. (See Euonymus on pages 87–89.)

Hedera Helix, Zone (V), English Ivy, is not one of the hardiest ground covers, but it can be grown in protected spots as far north as Massachusetts; however, in that latitude it sometimes winter kills. Ivy thrives in sun or in shade. It is less susceptible to winter injury when used as a ground cover than as a vine, and the foliage is much less apt to burn in winter if it is planted in a northern exposure. Northern gardeners will be wise to plant the *baltica* variety (Hedera Helix baltica), Zone IV, which is the hardiest type of English Ivy. Its leaves are slightly smaller than those of the regular type, and the veins are more prominently marked.

In addition to its usual uses as a ground cover, Ivy is excellent for climbing over tree stumps, boulders, walls, and trellises.

Propagation is no problem—indeed, the problem is usually to keep the planting within bounds. Shoots brought indoors for house decoration develop roots in water, and cuttings inserted in soil will strike root in a few days.

Mahonia Repens, Zone V, is a hardy creeping ground cover which grows ten to twelve inches high. *M. nervosa,* Zone V, is a shrubby ground cover that is from one to two feet tall. (See Mahonia on page 107.)

Pachistima Canbyi, Zone IV, Canby Pachistima, is an attractive small plant from the mountains of Virginia. It rarely exceeds eight to ten inches in height. Its evergreen foliage and dense habit make it of value for covering rocky slopes, for edging the shrubbery border, or for use wherever a low, neat ground cover is required.

Pachistima is hardy in all but the coldest parts of the country; it does well in sun or partial shade, and it likes a well-drained acid soil. The plants are increased by division of the old clumps, by layers, and by cuttings.

Another species *P. Myrsinites,* Zone V, is a low shrub eighteen inches or so high; its good foliage and form make it very desirable for partly shady situations.

Pachysandra Terminalis, Zone V, Japanese Spurge, is a member of the Box Family; it is a hardy plant and easy to grow, and it is one of the favorite plants of this group. It will grow in the sun but it definitely prefers a partly shady location. One of its important assets is its ability to hold banks. The author has successfully stopped erosion by covering a steep bank with this plant. This was done from cuttings taken in July after the new growth had hardened; the slips were cut two or three inches below the second whorl of leaves, plunged in a bucket of water for several hours, and then planted. By keeping them in water the tissues became filled with moisture, thus giving the slips a good start. The cuttings were planted two inches apart, and the stems were inserted in the soil sufficiently deep to bring the lower whorl of leaves level with the surface of the ground. In two weeks they were rooted and in a short time commenced to perform their intended function of holding the grade. Close planting is necessary for quick coverage, and it also provides shade which will make the plants more apt to succeed. It is of the greatest importance to keep the tops watered once or twice a day until wilting stops, but care must be taken to sprinkle the leaves lightly; otherwise the soil will become muddy and the cuttings will rot before they root.

Sometimes Pachysandra is attacked by a blight which causes brown spots on the leaves and stems. Discard badly infected plants; then spray with Ferbam or Captan. Thinning the planting from time to time will help to prevent this disease; another preventative is to maintain the vigor of the plants by feeding.

If the foliage loses some of its bright green color, a fertilizer will help to restore it. Dehydrated cow manure applied to the soil to the depth of about a quarter of an inch will be beneficial. Any soil of average fertility will meet the needs of this plant; however, if it is heavy in character, the texture should be improved with applications of sand and well-rotted manure.

Vases filled with Pachysandra cuttings make lovely winter greens for indoor decoration. Bring the cut shoots into the house before frost, and they will stay green all winter. When spring comes round, those that have rooted can be planted outdoors.

Sarcococca Hookeriana Humilis, Zone (V), is one of the most useful of all evergreen ground covers; unfortunately its hardiness cannot be depended upon north of Philadelphia. It is a slow-growing, spreading, dense plant twelve to fifteen inches high. It is not only of value as a ground cover, but because of its height and bushiness it is also a useful evergreen for planting under low windows and in spots where the planting areas are restricted. *Sarcococca* requires a shady place in which to grow; it is not demanding as to soil requirements. The fragrant, small white flowers bloom in early spring. Propagation is by division, seeds, and cuttings rooted in a shaded frame or under glass.

Skimmia Japonica, Zone VII?, is an unusually desirable ground cover. Its small white or pale pink flowers are followed by spikes of red berries. This plant is dioecious; consequently, for berry production, male and female plants are required for pollination purposes. *Skimmia* grows slowly—in the course of many years it will grow two and a half feet, with a spread equal to its height. It is easy to increase from cuttings taken any time. This shrublet is not a sun lover; choose a partly shady location for success. It prefers a light, sandy soil which contains peat moss.

Vinca Minor, Zone V, Periwinkle, Myrtle, is a native of Europe and has been extensively cultivated in gardens since ancient times. It is a trailing, evergreen plant that is hardy and easy to grow. Its glossy, small leaves and violet-blue flowers which appear in earliest spring make this plant a general favorite. It is always a joy to see these lovely blooms after the long winter months. *Vinca* likes a rich soil and will thrive in the shade or partial shade. It is a good choice to make for planting under trees, for carpeting foundation plantings, and for covering banks. If used for the latter purpose, the long trailing shoots should be pegged into the soil with thin pliable pieces of wire bent into a U shape; bringing the shoots into direct contact with the soil will cause the roots to form along the stems, and they will soon cover the bank and hold it securely. The best way to propagate Vinca is by division; it can also be increased by cuttings.

Part III

FLOWERING SHRUBS
FOR COLOR

Chapter X

Flowering Shrubs—Ab through Az

How gay are the flowering shrubs and how welcome their cheer after the long winter months! This invaluable group of plants contributes a pageant of color which brightens our gardens immeasurably. The majority of deciduous shrubs bloom in spring; however, some kinds flower later, which makes it possible by careful selection to enjoy blooms from early spring until autumn.

Deciduous shrubs are those that shed their leaves in the fall when the plants are dormant. The majority of them are easy to grow, and they provide a wealth of beauty. Use them with evergreens to lighten the solidity of an all-evergreen planting; in fact, it is by introducing both types of plant material that the ideal composition evolves.

The brilliant colors of the autumn foliage of many of these plants combine dramatically with the rich shades of the evergreens, weaving a colorful pattern before nature brings the season to a close. Before the last flowers have been gathered from the late-blooming shrubs, other bushes are already brightly decked with berries or fruits. Certain kinds, notably the bush Dogwoods, have vividly colored branches; while the stems of others, such as Kerria and Scotch Broom, remain green throughout the winter, thus carrying on the color theme and adding interest to the winter landscape.

137

Box and *Abelia grandiflora* give an attractive setting to the house.
Photographer, Paul E. Genereux.

As you read the pages that follow, bear in mind not only the effect of the flowers but also the charm that fall color will bring to your garden, and select at least a few shrubs conspicuous for their berries or for the bright autumnal tints of their foliage.

Abelia Grandiflora, Zone (V), Arbutus Bush, is an exceptionally ornamental, graceful shrub with small glossy leaves. During the summer and fall months it produces an abundance of delicate white flowers slightly tinted pink. Its comparatively low, compact habit of growth (three to six feet) makes it excellent for various purposes, such as foundation plantings, as a facer to the shrubbery border, or in combination with evergreens.

Abelia is easy to grow; if given a sunny spot in a protected location, it will thrive with little care. It prefers a well-drained, light soil to which a small amount of leaf mold or peat moss has been added. This species is semi-evergreen, and it is hardy as far north as New York. If planted in a well-protected place, it can be grown even farther north. The delicate fragrance of its flowers is especially pervading in damp, humid weather.

Propagation is easily accomplished by means of cuttings made in October. These are rooted under glass and wintered in a frame or indoors. In the South they can be kept outdoors.

Abelia floribunda is a beautiful Mexican species with pendulous bright rose flowers. It can be cultivated outdoors only south of Washington, D. C.

Abeliophyllum Distichum, Zone V, Korean Abelia-leaf, is a charming hardy shrub about five feet tall. In April its fragrant white flowers, borne in clusters, are very effective. When planted in the North, a sheltered location is advisable to protect the flower buds from injury. *Abeliophyllum* is an excellent bush for giving early spring bloom to the shrubbery border. It closely resembles Forsythia, but the flowers are smaller and are more abundant. It is not fastidious as to growing requirements; if given a well-drained location in the full sun, it will prosper. This shrub can be propagated by air-layers.

Acanthopanax Pentaphyllus, A. Sieboldianus, Zone IV, (*Aralia pentaphylla,*) is one of those accommodating shrubs to select for problem spots where nothing else will thrive. In smoky, dusty cities it grows on, regardless of impurities in the air. This plant is a good subject for screening purposes, and it takes root readily on rocky slopes. It is drought-

Abelia fills the deep corner by the steps. *Photographer, Paul E. Genereux.*

resistant and will stand partial shade. *Acanthopanax* attains a height of five to ten feet. Any well-drained soil that is reasonably fertile will meet the needs of this shrub. Propagation is easily done by means of either root or hardwood cuttings taken in the fall.

Aesculus Parviflora, Zone IV, Dwarf Horse Chestnut, will give an impressive effect in locations where a specimen plant is required. The erect panicles of creamy-white blooms are from eight to sixteen inches long and are borne in profusion during midsummer. It is not suitable for use in a small backyard; it is too heavy in its growth to be in the proper scale. *Aesculus* prefers loamy soil that is moist but well drained. In a sunny situation it will thrive; however, partial shade will not discourage its growth. Propagation is done by layerings, root cuttings, and by seeds stratified in the fall.

Amelanchier Canadensis, Zone IV, Shadbush, Shadblow, Service-berry, is an important species of this tree-like group of shrubs. The origin of the common name of Shadbush is attributed to the early settlers, be-cause its flowers usually expand when the shad is once more ascending the rivers. The delicate white flowers of this lovely shrub are well known to all those who wander through the woods in early spring. In small gar-dens it is very valuable wherever a light-growing shrub or small tree is required in sun or shade. Shadbush is admirable for places which are designed along informal lines.

It is entirely hardy and, when it is fully grown, often reaches a height of twenty-five feet. It succeeds in dry climates, and it will grow in prac-tically any soil. This shrub is increased by seeds gathered when ripe; they are stratified in the fall and sown the following spring. The plants can also be increased by root cuttings and by layers. *A. grandiflora* is an improved form.

Amorpha Fruticosa, False Indigo, is a spreading shrub of five to ten feet in height; it is hardy in the North. This is one of the less important plants, but it does come into its own when planted in moist situations— along the margin of streams, for instance. It will also succeed in dry soil. Although the foliage is rather scant, it gives an attractive and graceful effect. This shrub appears at its best when planted in masses rather than for the beauty of the individual plant. In sun or in partial shade it will thrive. The violet-purple flowers that bloom in May and June are not decorative. The supply can be increased by seeds, layers, suckers, and cuttings.

Front view of property before the planting was made.
Photographer, the Roches.

The approach to the house is always important; this well-thought-out planting scheme has greatly mellowed the house, and has created an atmosphere of warmth. A hedge of *Ilex crenata* screens the garage. The Shadbush (*Amelanchier*) in front of the house has been headed high in order to open the view. Note the variation in height and habit of growth that has been introduced in this excellent composition. *Owner, Mrs. John H. Locke. Courtesy The American Home. Photographer, the Roches.*

Back view of property prior to planting.

A dramatic change took place when this enchanting living area was surrounded with low-growing bushes, among which are *Cotoneasters* and *Azaleas*. The shrub border is the proper width to be in correct scale with the terrace, which is an important point to be considered. *Owner, Mrs. John H. Locke. Courtesy The American Home. Photographer, the Roches.*

Amorpha canescens, Zone II, Lead-plant, is native to various parts of this country. It is a handsome shrub about three feet high; because of its dwarf habit, it is suitable for the foreground of shrubbery borders or for foundation plantings. The blue flowers are borne in effective, compact spikes in June and July. It prefers well-drained, sunny locations.

Aralia Spinosa, Zone IV, Hercules' Club, is a bold, tree-like shrub fifteen to twenty feet tall. Since it has a coarse, heavy habit of growth, it is not suitable for use on small places. It gives the best effect when grown on spacious lawns. It can be planted advantageously as a specimen or to give privacy from a neighboring house. The bi-pinnate leaves sometimes measure two feet long, and the handsome creamy-white flowers are borne in clusters two feet long. Its blooming period is in mid-summer after most shrubs have finished flowering, and the large blooms and leaves give a spectacular effect.

Aralia is easy to transplant; it prefers a rather moist soil in which to grow, and it is not entirely hardy in far northern climates. It is indigenous to the southern states, where it is seen growing along the banks of streams and woodland borders; it likes a location in the light shade. Propagation is by seeds sown in spring, by root cuttings, and by suckers.

Aronia Arbutifolia, Zone V, Red Chokeberry, is a gay shrub for autumn effect with its profusion of red berry-like fruit. Its variety *brilliantissima* is even more effective when in berry. Strange as it may seem, the birds are not attracted to the fruit, notwithstanding the fact that the flavor is palatable; for this reason the berries persist on the branches well into the winter.

Aronia arbutifolia grows from six to ten feet tall; the white flower clusters appear in early spring. This shrub is a useful background plant for sunny or partially shady situations. It adapts itself to various kinds of soil but prefers one that is slightly moist.

Aronia melanocarpa, Zone IV, Black Chokeberry, is a more ornamental species in bloom and in foliage than *A. arbutifolia.* It grows to about four feet in height and produces purple-black berries which are not of much value because they soon fall from the branches. Still more desirable is *A. melanocarpa grandifolia;* it is taller, more vigorous, and has finer flowers and more lustrous foliage.

Aronia prunifolia, Zone IV, Purple Chokeberry, grows to about ten feet in height. The red-fruited kinds have more ornamental value.

Rhododendrons by the house, and masses of colorful *Azaleas* across the turf walk solve the problem of planting in the partial shade. *Photographer, H. Armstrong Roberts.*

Aronia is increased by seeds stratified in the fall, by greenwood cuttings rooted in a shaded frame, and by suckers and layers.

Azalea appears in all its glory in the congenial surroundings of the southern Appalachian Mountains, where masses of the yellow, orange, and red flowers of *Azalea calendulacea,* Flame Azalea, unfold in late spring, creating a spectacular display of color over the mountain-side. This variety is found as a hill dweller from New England southward. Among other kinds that abound in the woodlands are *Azalea canescens* (in the lower South), whose pale pink blooms diffuse the air with their fragrance in April and May; *A. vaseyi,* Pinkshell Azalea, which produces small pink flowers that open in early May; *A. nudiflora,* Pinxterbloom Azalea with flowers that appear in pink to nearly white about the middle of May; and *A. arborescens,* Sweet Azalea, whose flowers unfold late in June or July to spread their delicious fragrance. All of these love the cool dampness, the acid soil, and the partial shade of wooded places.

There are numerous Azaleas that add their beauty to the landscape. These include certain exceptionally fine Hybrids, such as the Ghent Hybrids, the Mollis Hybrids, and the more recent introduction—the Exbury Hybrids.

The various colors, heights, and habits of growth that Azaleas offer make them well adapted to many different uses; they are a lovely addition to practically any part of the planting composition. The native kinds are charming in naturalistic plantings. If you have a wooded lot where many flowers will not thrive, groups of native Azaleas here and there bordering the trees or planted among them are a happy solution. The hybrid kinds with their showy flowers are among the finest plant material available for formal use—in foundation plantings, as specimens, accent points, underplantings for trees, shrubbery borders, and to clothe a wall. Grown in masses on each side of the entrance to a property they provide a handsome effect. Entire gardens planted in Azaleas make a brilliantly colored picture. By a careful selection of varieties with different blooming seasons the flowers can be enjoyed over an extended period.

Soil Preparation. Azaleas are best planted in the spring or fall. The growing requirements of the deciduous kinds are similar to those of Rhododendrons and evergreen Azaleas. They like an acid soil, such as exists in woodlands, where year after year the fallen leaves decompose and provide the much needed acidity. In locations that do not offer such conditions the proper soil can be supplied by excavating the ground to the depth of eighteen inches and refilling the space with a mixture of 50 per cent leaf mold or peat moss and 50 per cent garden soil; a small amount of peat moss tucked in around the balled roots will give the plants a good start. If the surrounding soil is heavy in character, it should be ameliorated by spreading over it a good top-dressing of well-rooted cow manure and spading it under. Applications of sand incorporated in the soil will further lighten it.

Routine Care. A spring feeding with Cottonseed Meal or one of the special fertilizers on the market for Azaleas will give the plants a boost. A mulch of peat moss through the summer months and peat moss or oak leaves spread over the ground for winter protection will be admirable. During the growing season adequate watering should be given. Any faded flowers should be promptly removed to prevent the formation of seeds; it takes more energy for plants to produce seeds than to perform any other function.

Location. Azaleas particularly like partial shade; however, if the shade is on the light side the plants will be more floriferous. If they are given a sunny exposure, mulching the plants practically becomes a "must."

Propagation and Pests. See Chapter VIII.

The following species are among the most desirable for formal and informal plantings:

Azalea arborescens, Zone IV, (*Rhododendron arborescens*), Sweet Azalea, is a native species that grows nine feet tall. Its flowers are fragrant, and they appear late in June or early July. The rose-pink buds open into white flowers.

A. atlantica, Zone VI?, (*R. atlanticum*), is a low-growing kind eighteen inches high. Its native haunts extend from the southern part of Pennsylvania southward to South Carolina. As it will grow in sun or shade, and makes such a low growth, it fills many a nook in foundation plantings, in the foreground of shrubbery borders, and in various spots where a plant of its size is required. The fragrant flowers are white; some types are pink.

A. calendulacea, Zone V, (*R. calendulaceum*), Flame Azalea, develops into a shrub nine to ten feet in height, occasionally reaching fifteen feet. It is one of the most effective Azaleas for northern plantings. The flowers come in shades of yellow, orange, to red. This bush tolerates a sunny exposure. When many Azaleas have come and gone, *A. calendulacea* bursts into bloom in June; it is an extremely valuable native kind.

A. canescens, Zone VII?, (*R. canescens*), is a native type that grows in the South. Its pink to white blossoms that appear in April and May are delightfully fragrant. It is one of the taller growers, reaching a height of fifteen feet.

Exbury Hybrids are one of the signal accomplishments of recent hybridization. They are a cross between the Oriental, European, and American species, which has resulted in a new race of highly valuable Azaleas. They withstand zero temperatures and sunny or shady locations. The blooms are exceptionally effective and appear in almost every color; some of the individual flowers measure as much as four inches across. The blooming periods differ according to variety from May to early July. The plants are four to six feet in height and have a spread of four feet. In the fall the leaves turn brilliant red or yellow.

A. gandavense, (*R. gandavense*), Ghent Hybrids, are among the finest of all Azaleas and cover a wide range of color in yellow, orange, pink, and red. This race of Azaleas had its start in Ghent, Belgium, where a baker crossed a European species with some American forms. Later on, further hybridization was carried on in England, which resulted in producing the Ghent Hybrids of today. Most of these Azaleas are exceptionally hardy, and many survive temperatures in Maine as low as twenty degrees below zero. The plants grow six to ten feet high.

Glenn Dale Azaleas are a recent introduction; they have been widely acclaimed in this country and abroad. They produce large flowers in a variety of shades ranging from white to pink and red; however they have not all proved to be reliably hardy in the North; and when grown in the colder latitudes, they should be given protection. Since they have been freely hybridized, some growers report the leaves remain on the plant all winter.

A. japonica, (*R. japonicum*), Zone V, Japanese Azalea, comes to us from the mountains of Japan. It resembles *A. Kaempferi,* and its flowers in shades of yellow, orange, and flame contribute gay colors to any planting. It grows six feet tall.

A. Kaempferi, Zone IV, Torch Azalea, is another introduction from Japan, where its many colors make a brilliant display in the woodlands. The flower clusters appear in May in gorgeous shades of salmon pink to

A garden feature such as a bird bath, sundial or pool is set off with an attractive background planting. The *Azalea* in the picture is the pink-flowering variety *A. Schlippenbachi. Photographer, the Roches.*

salmon red. This hardy shrub develops into a bush about nine feet in height and five feet in width. It is excellent by pools in wooded areas and along streams. In evergreen plantings it is set off to best advantage where the vivid shades of the blooms will not conflict with the colors of other plant material.

A. mollis (*R. molle*), Zone (V), Mollis Hybrids, appear in a great variety of colors; their large blooms make them extremely valuable in the garden as accents, in background and foundation plantings, or wherever a hardy shrub five to six feet is required. They respond well to pruning, so that the height can be controlled, which makes them qualify for use wherever lower-growing shrubs are needed.

A. nudiflora, Zone III, (*R. nudiflorum*), Pinxterbloom Azalea, is a native plant widely distributed in woodlands in the eastern part of the country. Its small flowers appear in pink to nearly white about the middle of May. Unfortunately the foliage effect is rather scanty. It is an accommodating plant and will grow almost anywhere but prefers a partly shady location in moist soil.

A. rosea, Zone III, (*R. roseum,*) Roseshell Azalea, is much like *A. nudiflorum*. It has better blooms that are rose-pink in color, and they have a delightful fragrance like cloves.

A. Schlippenbachii, Zone IV, (*R. Schlippenbachii,*) Royal Azalea, is a hardy bush which attains a height of eight to ten feet, and has a spread of approximately three feet. Its large flowers come in pink and bloom early in May, continuing until June. Its foliage adds color to the autumn landscape in shades of yellow and red.

A. Vaseyi, Zone IV, (*R. Vaseyi,*) Pinkshell Azalea, is a native kind that produces small pink flowers that appear in early May. It is lovely for naturalizing along streams and in wooded areas. In the autumn the foliage turns bronzy red. In New England it grows about seven or eight feet tall, but in the more genial climate of South Carolina it reaches a height of fifteen feet. It can be kept down to almost any size by careful pruning.

A. viscosa, Zone III, (*R. viscosum*), Swamp Azalea, as its common name implies, is chiefly found in swampy land from Maine to South Carolina. Actually it does not require such conditions for its welfare; it will grow in any acid, fertile ground. The fragrance of its white flowers is delightful. It grows from five to ten feet; its flowers mark the end of the Azalea season in July. It is useful for informal plantings.

A. yodogava, Zone V, (*R. yedoense*), comes to us from Korea. It is a round-topped shrub which grows four to five feet tall. It is hardy, reliable, and free-flowering, bearing clusters of fragrant lilac to lilac-rose flowers in May. The color of the blooms does not combine well with most other colors.

To focus attention on the house, subordinate the planting by keeping it low. *Photographer, H. Armstrong Roberts.*

Before planting. *Photographer, Paul E. Genereux.*

The planting has tied the house to its surroundings. Outcroppings of boulders on the lawn have been softened with low-growing evergreens. Ground covers can also be used for this purpose. *Photographer, Paul E. Genereux.*

Chapter XI

Flowering Shrubs—B through C

Berberis, Barberry, with its brilliant berries and bright autumnal coloring of its leaves, adds an immense amount of cheer and interest to the fall landscape. In fact all season long this shrub with its attractive foliage and habit of growth makes it a welcome garden subject, whether it be for use as a specimen, a hedge, a shrubbery border, or a foundation planting.

The ease of its culture, together with its adaptability to a wide range of soils and locations, contributes to its general popularity. Barberry will stand some light shade, but the berry production and the autumnal tints of the foliage will not be so fine unless it is given a sunny situation. This shrub is not usually troubled with insect pests and diseases. Propagation is by seeds stratified in the fall and sown outdoors in the spring, or by cuttings of the new growth taken in June or July and rooted in a shaded frame. There are about 175 species, distributed in Asia, North Africa, Europe, and elsewhere. Some of the best of these are described below:

B. concinna, Zone VI?, is a low-growing species three feet tall, which comes to us from the Himalayas. The red berries and crimson foliage in fall make it most effective. It is deciduous or half-evergreen.

B. diaphana, Zone V, is a low, compact, spreading bush that grows about three feet high. Chinese in origin, its large yellow flowers are borne singly in May and early June. The drawback to this Barberry is its slowness in leafing out in spring.

B. koreana, Zone V, is an upright, strong-growing, dense shrub six feet tall. Its clusters of yellow flowers appear in May; these are followed by red berries. The foliage turns dark-red in autumn. This species is well adapted for use as a living fence.

B. mentorensis, Zone V, Mentor Barberry, has been produced by crossing *B. Thunbergii* and *B. Julianae.* The resulting plant is a hardy, ornamental, upright-growing shrub seven feet tall. It requires little or no pruning. This bush is excellent for hedges and foundation plantings, and it succeeds well in city yards. It is a sturdy, drought-resistant form, and is said to be ever-green in some parts of the country. The blooming period is in May; the yellow flowers are followed by dark-red berries.

B. Thunbergii, Zone V, Japanese Barberry, is the most familiar and most extensively planted of all Barberries. It is very dense in its habit of growth, which makes it suitable for hedges. If allowed to grow unchecked it becomes six to seven feet tall. The fall foliage and the berries are a bright scarlet. A variety of this species, *atropurpurea,* is a red-leaved form, which is difficult to use in the garden because of its color. The variety *Truehedge Columnberry* is an erect, narrow-growing type that is also good for hedge work.

B. vernae, Zone V, is a dense shrub six feet high, with arching branches and bright yellow flowers followed by red berries.

B. vulgaris, Zone III, Common Barberry, is of European origin. It is a very decorative form and grows to eight feet. Its berries are a bright coral-red. Since it is a host to the wheat rust, its use in localities where wheat is grown is prohibited. However, in other regions it is a lovely species with effective, drooping yellow flowers.

B. Wilsonae, Zone (V), is a Chinese species which in general resembles the Japanese Barberry (*B. Thunbergii*). It is not as hardy as the latter, nor is it as large or as heavy a plant. In the fall its coloring attracts attention with the coral-red berries and the foliage that turns red. This shrub is deciduous or half-evergreen.

Buddleia Davidi, Zone (V), Butterfly-bush, Summer Lilac, is highly valued for its long, effective flowers that are borne profusely; if the faded blooms are removed promptly, the flowers will continue to appear for several weeks. As its name implies, its sweetly scented blossoms are a mecca for butterflies. Varieties of Buddleia come with white, lilac, purple, or pink flowers; it is one of the most valuable of all summer-blooming shrubs. It sprang into popularity about the beginning of the century when marked improvements were introduced. The original plant was found growing in China in 1869 by a French Jesuit priest. After World War I, it was very much in demand in France, especially in Verdun where it was named the "Flower of the Ruins."

This shrub likes a sunny, well-drained location in soil that is rich. An annual growth of about four feet is made; therefore each spring before growth starts it should be cut back to about one foot from the ground. As a matter of fact, in severe winters the bush will winter-kill to the ground; however, new growth soon replaces the loss unless the temperatures are sufficiently low to kill the roots. Old canes should be cut out at ground level to maintain a plentiful supply of young shoots, which are the most floriferous. *Buddleia* is not a hardy shrub and is not often seen growing north of Philadelphia. The habit of growth is rather ungainly, but when it is used in the shrubbery border where it is surrounded by other shrubs, this defect is less conspicuous.

Propagation is best done by cuttings of the mature wood taken in fall and kept through the winter in a cool, frost-proof room.

Buddleia alternifolia, Zone V, is the hardiest species. It blooms on wood of the previous season's growth. Unlike *B. Davidi,* Zone (V), this shrub should not be pruned until the flowering period is over. It is a large shrub, twelve feet high, with spreading branches. This bush qualifies for specimen planting or for use in the shrub border. The fragrant lilac flowers appear in June.

Callicarpa, Beauty-berry, is grown chiefly for its lilac or violet berries, which are very unusual and decorative; unfortunately they are not long lasting, as the birds usually denude the bushes of its fruit before the season is far spent.

It is not reliably hardy north of Philadelphia; farther north it is apt to die down to the ground. However, in the spring new shoots appear which bear blooms and fruit the same season. This shrub should be planted in a protected location, in sun or partial shade.

Propagation is by seeds, layers, and cuttings made from hardwood or growing wood; the latter are rooted in a shaded frame.

C. Bodinieri Giraldii, Zone (V), grows to ten feet; its pink blooms are followed by violet fruit.

C. japonica, Zone (V), grows five feet tall; its flowers are light pink, and it produces violet berries.

C. dichotoma, (*C. purpurea*), Zone (V), has lilac-violet fruit, and it grows to four feet.

Calluna Vulgaris, Zone IV, Heather, is an attractive low-growing shrub one to two feet high. It is found growing along the East Coast. It makes a useful ground cover for rocky or sandy soils. Unfortunately it is not a long-lived plant and has to be replaced every few years. In regions where the ground is covered with snow throughout the winter it seems to live for a longer time. *Calluna* requires an acid soil in a well-drained location. It grows well in a mixture of one-third each of oak leaf mold or peat moss, sand, and topsoil. In earliest spring a severe annual pruning will improve the blooms and help to overcome the straggly growth. Heather will stand a little shade, but a sunny situation is decidedly preferable.

The plants can be increased from cuttings of the young growth taken in early fall and rooted under glass. The flowers that appear in mid-summer are available in white, pink, or red forms.

Calycanthus Floridus, Zone IV, Carolina Allspice, Sweet Shrub, Strawberry Bush, is a hardy shrub which attains a height of six to nine feet. It was widely used in early Colonial days—in fact, George Washington and Thomas Jefferson included it in their gardens. Because of its fragrance and its association with the past, it is still a welcome plant in the gardens of today. The flowers are rather curious-looking and are chocolate-brown in color; the leaves, the bark, and the blooms are all fragrant. It is useful in the shubbery border or for planting close to the outdoor living area where its sweet scent can be enjoyed. It thrives in sunny or partly shady locations.

Strawberry Bush prefers a rich, moist, but well-drained soil. It is not overly easy to transplant, but when it becomes well established it is a persistent grower. It is also long-lived and practically free from insect pests and diseases. *Calycanthus* is easily propagated by division or by layers made during the summer. The newer strains carried by nurserymen seem to be losing the fragrance of the original type; therefore if you have a friend who is fortunate enough to have the old-fashioned strain, try to obtain a division of the plant.

When houses are built at close range, an unbroken lawn area mutually shared gives a greater sense of space. The foundation plantings of the different houses are varied, thus avoiding the monotonous effect of repetition. *Photographer, Paul E. Genereux.*

Caragana Arborescens, Zone II, Pea-tree, is a large shrub which sometimes grows to a height of twenty feet. The small, yellow, pea-shaped flowers are borne profusely in spring, but they are not particularly showy. The habit of the bush is stiff and the foliage is not luxuriant. Its chief use is as a background shrub. In the prairie sections of the Northwest it is an excellent bush for hedge work.

The Pea-tree is hardy, easy to transplant, and prefers a light soil in warm, sunny locations. The stock can be increased by seeds and layers. A weeping variety, *pendula,* is an attractive form, especially when it is grafted and grown as a standard.

C. microphylla, Zone III, grows four to six feet high; it is spreading and open in its growth. Its flowers are yellow, and it has finely divided foliage.

C. pygmaea, Zone III, is a low-growing shrub from one to three feet high. The flowers are yellow, and the leaves are finely divided.

Caryopteris Incana, Zone VII, Blue-beard, Blue Spirea, is an attractive small shrub which does not usually exceed two to three feet in height. It is one of those bushes that can be tucked into odd corners, and as a facer to taller growing plants it fills a real need. It also can be included in the herbaceous border, where it ties in well with the planting as accent points, giving substance to the perennials. The pretty lavender-blue flowers are generously produced over a period of several weeks, commencing in late summer. This is a real asset because it comes at a season when few shrubs are blooming.

In common with Buddleia, Blue Spirea is apt to die back severely in the winter; however, new shoots grow quickly from the roots in spring. If winter does not do the needed pruning, it will then be necessary to cut the plant down close to the ground in early spring. When the pruning is done at that time, no bloom will be sacrificed because the flowers form on wood of the current season's growth.

A sunny, protected situation in well-drained, light soil will provide the best growing conditions. Propagation is by seeds sown in spring, or by cuttings of the ripe wood taken in late summer or early fall and rooted under glass. There are white and pink flowering varieties of this shrub, but the lavender-blue forms are preferable. The variety Blue Mist is a lovely soft blue shade, another favorite is Heavenly Blue, which is a deeper blue color.

Cephalanthus Occidentalis, Zone IV, Button bush, is a hardy shrub which grows to a height of twelve feet. It is not suited to small gardens, but comes into its own when planted on spacious lawns or on wooded lots. It is also adapted for planting in swampy ground or along the margins of streams. Although this plant grows in wet locations, it grows successfully in practically any soil. The fragrant flowers which appear in summer are in the form of curious balls that are crowded with many cream-colored flowers. These are filled with a nectar that is loved by the bees. The plants can be started from seeds or from cuttings of the ripe wood taken in summer.

Cercis Canadensis, Zone IV, Judas-tree, Redbud, is a showy, tree-like shrub which covers itself with myriads of small rosy-magenta flowers in early spring. Some seasons it blooms with the white Dogwood (*Cornus florida*) which sets off the color of its flowers. Since its blooms do not blend with the spring flowering plants, it should be provided with a background of greens. It can also be planted as a specimen. If this shrub is properly placed, it is a good subject for small properties. The white variety *alba* will give the touch of white that brings out other colors to the best advantage.

Judas-tree will stand shade, but when planted in wooded areas it becomes tall and spindly. In open, sunny locations this shrub usually remains about ten feet high. A rich, sandy soil suits it best. Transplanting is difficult and should be done in spring; young bushes stand being moved better than the older shrubs. Propagation is by seeds, softwood cuttings, and air layers.

C. chinensis, Zone VI, is not as hardy as the *canadensis,* and when it is planted as far north as New York it does not often exceed four feet in height. It grows in sun or partial shade; its foliage is glossier and its flowers are a little deeper in color than those of the *canadensis*.

Chaenomeles Japonica, Zone IV, (Cydonia japonica), Japanese Quince, is one of the loveliest early flowering spring shrubs in cultivation. It is a rather low, dense, and spreading bush about three feet high. The gay orange-red or red flowers which crowd the branches burst into a blaze of bloom before the leaves unfold. Japanese Quince should be planted as a specimen where it has ample space in which to develop; the bloom effect will be improved if it is given a sheltered spot. It is not fastidious as to soil requirements, but a sunny location is a requisite.

Before planting. *Photographer, Paul E. Genereux.*

Shrubs and flowers combine to make a colorful outdoor living area.
Photographer, Paul E. Genereux.

Since the importation of European varieties, San Jose scale is not as serious a pest as it was formerly. If scale appears, it can be eliminated with a dormant spray of either Lime-sulphur or oil. Blight sometimes attacks the plants; when this occurs, all affected parts must be cut off at once and burned.

Chaenomeles is a difficult shrub for the home gardener to increase; however, it can be propagated by stem or root cuttings.

C. lagenaria, Zone IV, Flowering Quince, is an exceptionally decorative shrub which grows to a height of six feet. Named varieties come in lovely shades of apple blossom pink, coral pink, white, and red. The large greenish-yellow fruit is distinctive and can be used for making jellies and preserves. It is a good shrub for informal hedge work. The best means of propagation is by air-layers.

C. japonica var. alpina is a dwarf, spreading form eighteen inches high; it has orange-red flowers.

C. sinensis, Zone (V), Chinese Quince, produces pale pink flowers; in the fall the leaves turn red.

Chionanthus Virginicus, Zone IV, Fringe-tree, is a tree-like shrub which sometimes reaches thirty feet. It is especially valued for the beauty of its fragrant, pendulous panicles of white flowers which appear in late May or June. The leaves are so slow in leafing out in spring that the shrub appears to have been winter-killed. The foliage becomes bright yellow in the autumn. The Fringe-tree is splendid for use as a specimen and for providing privacy; its dimensions make it a good shrub for filling a deep corner. The flowers of the male plant surpass those of the female in decorative value; the flower panicles of the former are longer, measuring eight inches in length. However, the male plant lacks the pendulous blue fruits produced by the female. In common with most of the Hollies, a male plant is required for berry production.

The Fringe-tree will thrive best in a bright, sunny location; it prefers soil that is fertile and light. Northern gardeners will do well to plant this shrub in a sheltered situation and to give it winter protection. This beautiful tree was planted in the gardens of Washington and Jefferson; the latter called it the "fringe" or "snow-drop tree."

Propagation is by seeds stratified in the fall, by layers, and by cuttings.

C. retusus, Zone V, is a hardy Chinese species whose flower panicles are shorter than those of *C. virginicus.* It attains a height of twenty feet.

Clethra Alnifolia, Zone III, Summersweet, a native along the coast from Maine to Florida, is an inhabitant of moist or marshy land. It eventually reaches a height of ten feet. The fragrant, erect clusters of white flowers appear in midsummer when few shrubs are in bloom. The sweet scent is enjoyable in the shrubbery border and also indoors when the flowers are used for cut-flower arrangements. *Clethra* is among the shrubs that grow successfully at the seashore.

Although this bush will grow in various soils, it shows a preference for moist, light ground that has been enriched with oak leaf mold or peat moss. It is not often troubled with insect pests or diseases; however, if it is planted in a dry situation, red spider is likely to attack it. The supply can be increased by division of the clumps, by layering, by seeds, and by cuttings made from the growing wood.

C. alnifolia rosea is an attractive variety with pink buds.

C. barbinervis, Zone (V), Japanese Clethra, grows thirty feet high and is very effective when in bloom. The flowers are not as highly scented as those of *C. alnifolia.* It is less subject to red spider than the latter.

* Cornus Florida, Zone IV, Flowering Dogwood, is one of our finest native flowering trees. In May the beautiful so-called "flowers" (which botanically speaking are bracts) are extremely showy. When summer passes, and with it the luxuriance of the growing season, it still delights us with the brilliant crimson tints of its foliage and its bright red berries. The variety *Xanthocarpa* is a yellow-fruited form.

This tree makes an outstanding specimen for lawn plantings on both small and large places. It is striking when combined with evergreens which provide an ideal setting for the spring flowers and the autumn coloring.

Dogwood grows in the sun or partial shade; it succeeds in practically any well-drained soil; however, it responds favorably to one that is fertile and slightly acid. The best planting season is in early spring before growth starts. In cold climates the flower buds sometimes winter-kill, but in a protected location this is less apt to occur.

Unfortunately Dogwood is subject to some pests, one of which is the borer. A good preventive measure is to spray with Malathion or .50 per cent wettable DDT powder, which should be applied the third week

* It is included because of its popularity. See Author's Note.

The Flowering Dogwood and evergreens add greatly to the interest of this rock garden. *Photographer, Paul E. Genereux.*

in May; two or three additional sprayings at two-week intervals will give good protection. If borers already exist, a fumigant such as Carbon Bisulphide can be used to eliminate them. This should be dropped into the borer holes with a medicine dropper and the holes closed immediately with soap or adhesive to shut in the deadly fumes. Carbon Bisulphide is highly explosive; no lighted match or cigarette should come near it.

Crown canker is another troublesome pest. It can be recognized by loss of leaves and a die-back of the crown; the remaining foliage becomes sparse, small, and yellowish. The remedy is to scrape off every bit of discolored wood and to remove one and a half inches of the healthy wood surrounding the diseased portion. When the wound has been thoroughly cleaned, apply orange shellac to all exposed surfaces. Fertilize and prune the plant to build up its vigor and resistance. Be watchful for scale; if it appears, the bushes sholud be sprayed when dormant with an oil preparation. This should only be used when the temperature is between 40 and 65 degrees; otherwise the shrub may be burned if the oil becomes separated. Apply the spray early in the morning and do not use it after the buds have begun to open. One spraying will be sufficient. A dormant spray of Lime-sulphur is an alternative; however, it has the drawback of discoloring stone, brick, and paint. Whichever spray is applied, follow carefully the manufacturer's directions. Sometimes in late spring a nicotine spray will be efficacious.

Cornus florida is propagated by seeds sown in the fall in a frame. The pink flowering form, *C. florida rubra,* cannot be depended upon to come true to color if grown from seeds; this kind is usually grafted or budded. The home gardener who wishes to increase his supply can try air-layering, which has been successfully accomplished.

The shrub Dogwoods can be multiplied by layers and by cuttings taken in the fall; others are increased by division. The various species of this group are well adapted for use in naturalistic and informal plantings. Some of them, notably *C. alba sibirica,* are splendid subjects for the mixed border. They grow to a height of approximately ten feet or more. *C. alba sibirica,* Siberian Dogwood, bears numerous clusters of small white flowers in May, which are followed by bluish-white fruits. Because of its berries and bright red branches, this shrub is an exceptionally distinctive one for fall and winter effect. The young wood is the most colorful; therefore in order to keep up a supply of new growth, pruning is an

important part of the culture. This advice holds good for all of the Dogwoods that are principally grown for the winter effect of their branches.
C. Amomum, Zone V, Silky Dogwood, is of particular interest for the
winter landscape because of its bright red branches; however, these are
not as ornamental as those of *C. alba sibirica.* This shrub is hardy, long-
lived, and a fairly rapid grower. Its yellowish flowers do not appear until
June; they are followed by blue or whitish fruits. *C. Amomum* thrives
best in moist or wet soils and requires ample space for its full development.

C. Kousa, Zone V, Japanese Flowering Dogwood, is a tall shrub or small
tree indigenous to the Orient; it is one of the finest of the Dogwoods. The
white flowers that appear in June after the shrub is in full leaf are almost
as decorative as those of the native Flowering Dogwood. The red berries
that resemble strawberries, together with the red autumnal foliage, contribute interest to the fall effect. It reaches a height of twenty feet.

**A Dogwood strategically placed breaks an otherwise uninteresting line
of wall; the house foundation is further softened with lower-growing
shrubbery. *Photographer, Paul E. Genereux.***

C. mas, Zone IV, Cornelian Cherry, is a tall, broad shrub of European origin. The clusters of yellow flowers are especially conspicuous because they appear in early April before the shrub is in leaf. The foliage is glossy and turns scarlet in the fall; this attribute combined with its red fruit makes it a good candidate for autumn color. A young plant can be moved without difficulty. It is a long-lived shrub, and fairly free from insects and diseases.

C. racemosa, Zone IV (*C. paniculata*), Gray Dogwood, is well suited for background and informal plantings. Its white blooms appear in June or July and are followed by white fruits borne on red stems; these contrasting colors combined with the gray branches give quite an unusual touch to the fall and winter garden.

C. stolonifera, Zone II, Red-Osier Dogwood, is still another species that is chiefly valued for the winter coloring of its crimson branches. Suckers are produced freely, and the shrub is dense and spreading in its habit. It is a useful plant for situations in moist soil, for which it has definite preference. The white flowers that appear the latter part of May are followed by white, pea-like fruits. *C. stolonifera flaviramea,* Yellow-twig Dogwood, is a variety with yellow colored branches. The stems of the variety *C. s. nitida* remain green all winter.

Corylopsis, Winter-hazel, is one of the choicest of the early spring flowering shrubs, and it is well-deserving of the best care. It is not a very hardy bush and should be given a protected spot in either sun or light shade. The dainty, graceful, fragrant pale-yellow flowers are always a joy. Corylopsis thrives in rich, moist, acid soil; it is propagated by layers and seeds. *C. glabrescens,* Zone V, (*C. Gotoana*), is the hardiest species; it does not ordinarily exceed six feet in height; this bush has a broad spread. *C. pauciflora,* Zone VI, also grows to six feet.

Cotinus Coggygria (see Rhus coggygria, page 212.)

Cotoneaster is an interesting, ornamental group of shrubs of great value to the home gardener. The different species vary widely in appearance and habit of growth; some are upright bushes four to twelve feet in height, and others, such as *C. horizontalis* and *C. adpressa,* are prostrate in habit. The taller growing forms are decorative in the shrub border, for foundation plantings, or to give background to a feature such as a garden pool; whereas the prostrate forms are excellent for the rock garden and for covering slopes. The foliage of many of the species color brilliantly in the fall. While the majority are not showy in bloom, the large white flowers of *C. hupehensis* and *C. multiflora* are very effective.

Cotoneaster will grow satisfactorily in almost any soil that is well drained; it fails to thrive in shady, moist situations. Propagation is by seeds or by layers. There are some evergreen kinds which can be increased by cuttings of the half-ripe wood. These are made in August and are rooted in a shaded frame.

Fire-blight is one of the enemies to which this plant is susceptible; prompt removal of the diseased parts is essential; prune the branches

A house devoid of shrubbery is unwelcoming and bleak. *Photographer, J. Horace McFarland Company.*

back to healthy wood, making the cuts at least one foot below the affected portions, and paint the wounds with orange shellac. If scale appears, spray the bushes in early spring before growth starts, using a dormant spray of Lime-sulphur or oil. During the growing season Nicotine-sulphate is safe to apply, as it will not damage the leaves; however, it is not as efficacious as a dormant spray.

Some of the best garden forms of *Cotoneaster* are as follows:
C. adpressa, Zone IV, is a charming, small-leaved, decorative species with pink flowers. It grows close to the ground, and its stems frequently

This is a good example of the striking improvement that was brought about by an attractive foundation planting. The low evergreens on the right of the picture are *Taxus repandens;* these are used as facers to the taller shrubs. *Photographer, J. Horace McFarland Company.*

take root as they spread. This plant is useful for covering slopes and also as a rock garden subject. The red berries and the dark red color of the autumn foliage give a gay note to the fall effect.

C. apiculata, Zone IV, is a spreading, handsome shrub with pink flowers, followed by large, cranberry-like, red fruit.

C. bullata, var. floribunda, is a shrub five to six feet high. The pinkish flowers are followed by red berries that give an exceptionally fine display.

C. Dielsiana, Zone (V), is a dense shrub six to ten feet tall. Its slender, graceful branches are covered with showy red berries.

C. divaricata, Zone V, grows five to six feet in height. It is a desirable shrubby form, with effective red berries and red foliage in the fall; this is one of the best species.

C. Francheti, Zone VI?, is a semi-evergreen, upright, dense shrub which grows eight to ten feet in height. The berries that appear in the fall are orange-red in color.

C. horizontalis, Zone IV, is another semi-evergreen type and is perhaps the best known of the group. Its low, dense, spreading branches qualify it for use as a ground cover. Its bright red berries and scarlet leaves in fall make this a colorful plant for autumn display. The variety *perpusilla* is more dwarf than the type.

C. hupehensis, Zone IV, is an effective shrub in bloom; its white flowers that are followed by red berries make it an attractive species. It grows to six feet in height.

C. multiflora, Zone V, has a spreading habit of growth and becomes six feet high. It is one of the most floriferous of the *Cotoneasters,* and it makes quite a show when its white flowers are in bloom in May. These are followed by red fruit. The variety *calocarpa* bears larger red berries and in greater profusion than the type.

C. racemiflora soongorica, Zone III, grows eight feet tall. It has unusually ornamental red fruit.

C. salicifolia var. floccosa, Zone (V), is half-evergreen and reaches a height of fifteen feet. The white flowers appear about mid-June and are followed by red fruit. This shrub develops into an unusually graceful form with narrow leaves.

Shrub forms of *Cotoneaster* with black fruits are *C. nitens,* Zone IV, *C. melanocarpa,* Zone IV, and *C. lucida,* Zone IV. Naturally these species are not as colorful as the red-fruited kinds.

Cytisus Scoparius, Zone V, Scotch Broom, is a hardy shrub which sometimes grows about ten feet high. It is a useful plant for covering banks in well-drained, dry, poor, gravelly soil; as a matter of fact, *Cytisus* does not thrive in rich ground. An exposure in the full sun is a requisite for success. Its bright yellow flowers that contrast with the green stems bring a cheerful display in the planting scheme. An annual pruning immediately after the blooming season will help to keep the shrub more shapely. Inasmuch as large specimens are difficult to transplant, it is best to purchase young plants. Propagation is by layers, seeds, or cuttings of the growing wood taken in summer. These are rooted under glass.

C. nigricans, Zone V, is not as vigorous a grower. It is approximately four feet high, and its flowers contribute bright yellow to the color scheme wherever it is planted.

Dwarf forms of Broom that grow about one foot high are *C. Ardoinii,* Zone VII; *C. kewensis* and *C. albus,* Zone V; *C. Beanii,* Zone V, grows to sixteen inches, and *C. decumbens,* Zone V, to eight inches. These are all good for the rockery and for tucking into restricted spaces; all can withstand zero temperatures, with the exception of *C. Ardoinii,* which cannot endure much frost.

Before the property was landscaped.
*Owner, J. L. Berrall. Photographer,
George B. Biggs, Inc.*

Shrubs have transformed this place into an inviting spot. The *Deutzia* on the extreme right ornaments the entrance with its profusion of white flowers. *Photographer, the Roches.*

Chapter XII

Flowering Shrubs—D through H

Daphne Cneorum, Zone IV, Rose Daphne, Garland Flower, is a charming low-growing shrub with lovely fragrant, pink flowers in spring; its growth is inclined to be straggly; however, this can be partly corrected by pinching out the tips of the shoots after bloom. This species is classified as an evergreen, but it is definitely a borderline evergreen as far north as Philadelphia and cannot be depended upon to give a good winter effect. It is a favorite plant for the rock garden and is also useful for edging purposes or to fill in where a shrublet eight to ten inches high is required. It seems to do well in both alkaline and acid soils, and it thrives in sunny, well-drained locations. If it is exposed to the winter sun, the leaves are likely to burn; however, a light veiling of straw or evergreen boughs will help to prevent this discoloration. The best way to increase the plants is by simple layerage; mound layerings can also be made.

D. Burkwoodii, D. Somerset, is a broad shrub which attains a height of about five feet; its faintly scented flesh-pink flowers are quite effective. It is a good shrub for a mixed border planting, where the more luxuriant bushes give it substance.

D. Genkwa, Zone (V), is a choice small bush about two or three feet high. Its fragrant lilac flowers appear in spring before the leaves unfold, and they make an exceptionally lovely effect. It is attractive for foundation plantings or in restricted spaces on the terrace or patio. A little pampering may be needed until it becomes well established, but it well deserves the best of care.

D. Mezereum, Zone IV, February Daphne, is an upright, rather stiff shrub three or four feet tall. In earliest spring its fragrant violet flowers burst into bloom. Unfortunately it is subject to scale.

Deutzia is an easy shrub to grow and thrives in moist, well-drained soil which contains organic matter. It prefers a sunny location, but will tolerate light shade. When the flowering season is over, the bushes should be pruned in order to thin out the old wood; this induces new growth, which is important because the young branches flower the most profusely. The stock can be multiplied readily by greenwood or hardwood cuttings. In spring the bushes are covered with white or pinkish blooms. These are its chief attraction, as at other seasons the plants lack interest. The foliage effect is dull, and it does not color in the fall.

D. gracilis, Zone IV, Slender Deutzia, is a charming species. It is low-growing, seldom being over three feet high. It forms a compact bush and is very floriferous; the white flowers usually appear at tulip time and add their shower of bloom to the many-colored bulbs.

D. Lemoinei, Zone IV, is a large, spreading shrub six feet tall, and it has a more vigorous habit of growth than the *gracilis.* A variety of this species, *D. Lemoinei compacta,* is a hardy, low-growing bush with an abundance of white flowers.

Other desirable Deutzias are *D. grandiflora,* Zone V; *D. candelabrum* (one of the most effective in bloom); and *D. magnifica,* Zone (V). All of these grow approximately six feet in height. *D. rosea eximia* has pinkish flowers, and *D. scabra candidissima* is a white double-flowering form.

Dipelta Floribunda, Zone V, comes to us from China. It is a hardy shrub. Ordinarily it does not exceed six or eight feet, but sometimes attains a height of fifteen feet under favorable conditions. It is ornamental when in bloom; the fragrant pale-pink flowers are borne in clusters along the stems in May or June. *Dipelta* prefers a location in the full sun; it grows best in any good moist garden soil. Propagation is by cuttings taken from the growing wood, or from the mature wood in the fall.

A hedge of Spirea Vanhouttei gives seclusion from the public road.
Owner, J. L. Berrall. Photographer, the Roches.

Elaeagnus, with its distinctive silvery green foliage and its ornamental berries, is an unusual shrub to introduce in the planting. There are various species distributed in parts of North America, Europe, and Asia. The evergreen kinds are not hardy; however, various deciduous forms can be grown successfully in the North. The flowers are inconspicuous, but they are delightfully fragrant. A sunny location in practically any well-drained soil will meet the needs of this easy-to-grow shrub. The supply can be increased by cuttings made in late summer or fall, and also by layers.

E. angustifolia, Zone II, Oleaster, Russian Olive, has been named the Tree of Paradise by the Portuguese because of the sweet fragrance of its blossoms. The Russian Olive is a large bush fifteen to twenty feet in height; it is best used as a specimen; however, plants that are kept compact by pruning serve as useful shrubs for screening purposes and for giving privacy to the outdoor living area. The silvery underside of the leaves is an added attraction; the small silver flowers (yellow inside) are followed by yellowish fruit. This plant is a good subject for seashore gardens and city yards.

E. commutata, Zone II, Silver-berry Elaeagnus, is well named because of its silvery foliage and silver berries. It grows about six feet tall. The yellow flowers are silvery on the outside and are fragrant.

E. multiflora, Zone IV, is a shrub eight feet high, with leaves that are silvery on the undersides. The fragrant blooms which appear in May are followed by red fruits. This bush is an ornamental type for home gardens; it is useful for foundation plantings or for a mixed shubbery border. It is easy to transplant and is rarely troubled by insects and diseases.

Enkianthus Campanulatus, Zone IV, Redvein Enkianthus, an enchanting shrub of Japanese origin, should be more generally planted. Its light habit of growth makes it a splendid bush for small grounds. It is adapted for use either as a specimen or to soften the corner of the house. Its graceful clusters of creamy-yellow, bell-shaped flowers are tinged with red, and when they bloom in May, they always attract attention. With the arrival of the autumn days the leaves turn a bright red. In this country the species does not ordinarily exceed a height of ten feet.

Enkianthus belongs to the same family as Rhododendrons; in common with them it needs a moist, well-drained, acid soil that is well supplied with oak leaf mold or peat moss. It will grow in sun or partial shade.

Propagation is by seeds, layers, and cuttings of the growing wood made in the summer; it is also increased by air-layers.

E. perulatus, Zone V, grows approximately six feet high. It is an ornamental plant with white flowers in drooping clusters that appear in May. Both kinds of *Enkianthus* combine well with groupings of broad-leaved evergreens and give contrast in form and foliage.

Erica, Heath, is classified as an evergreen. However, in the colder climates it is a borderline shrub; the foliage gives a very poor effect in winter. It comprises a valuable and interesting group of plants which vary in height from a few inches to twenty feet in the tree species. The Heaths are well suited to naturalizing, and they are charming for rock gardens, for bordering Rhododendron and Azalea plantings, and for ground covers. In the more genial climates, such as the Pacific Northwest, it is possible to enjoy their color over quite an extended period. By careful selection of varieties, flowers can be had practically all-year-round.

The Heaths require an acid soil and a location that is sunny and quite dry; unlike most plants, they do not thrive in rich ground. If the plants become straggly, they should be cut back close to the ground. This will not only renovate them but will improve their shapeliness. It must be done in spring, and it is the only kind of pruning that is necessary. New plants can be made from cuttings taken during the summer and rooted in a shaded frame, or by layering branches that grow close to the ground—in fact, these often root naturally.

E. arborea, Zone VII, is the Tree Heath, which grows to twenty feet in milder climates. Its fragrant white flowers are produced abundantly.

E. carnea, Zone V, Spring Heath, is a delightful early-comer, blooming in March or April. Its pretty deep-rose flowers even appear in the rigorous climate of New England; varieties can be had in white or purple. It is a low-grower, only one foot high.

E. ciliaris, Zone VII?, Fringed Heath, grows to about eighteen inches; it bears rosy-purple flowers in summer. The white flowering variety *alba* is especially attractive.

E. darleyensis is a shrub three feet high. Its light lilac blooms are in flower from November to March.

E. vagans, Zone V, Cornish Heath, is a summer flowering plant one foot high. Varieties come in white, red, and pink-purple.

Euonymus, Spindle Tree, in its deciduous forms has outstandingly good foliage that colors brilliantly in the autumn. The flowers are not conspicuous, but the fruits are very ornamental. (See page 87.)

Euonymus is not difficult to grow; it transplants easily and does well in most soils. The chief difficulty with this plant is its susceptibility to scale. This pest must be watched for and eradicated before it takes complete charge. Sometimes it becomes so serious it is necessary to cut the bushes back to the ground and start them anew. A dormant oil spray is efficacious in combatting this pest. (See page 87.)

E. alata, Zone III, Winged Spindle-tree, is a hardy, handsome shrub both in form and foliage. It grows into a broad, compact bush about nine feet high; its corky, horizontal branches make it particularly distinctive. Its leaves turn a lovely shade of rosy-red in the fall, and it is comparatively immune to scale. *E. alata compacta* is a very desirable form that is hardy, dense, and lower-growing than the type. It is an extremely useful plant for hedge work.

E. americana, Zone VI, Strawberry-bush, is an upright shrub growing to eight feet; the fruit is rose or reddish. It is not a popular kind for the home garden because it lacks the high autumn coloring of the other species.

E. Bungeana, Zone IV, is a good choice for the gardener who is looking for a fast-growing shrub. It reaches a height of eighteen feet and is a good bush for background or boundary plantings. Its variety *semipersistens* is superior; its light green foliage and yellowish or pinkish fruits persist on the branches into the winter.

E. europaea, Zone III, European Spindle-tree, reaches a height of twenty feet and is especially valued for its colorful fruit. The leaves turn purplered, and the fruit is red to pink.

E. nana, Zone II, Dwarf Euonymus, grows three feet high and bears pink fruit.

E. obovata, Zone III, Running Strawberry-bush, is a very hardy shrub one foot high. It grows close to the ground, and the branches that contact the soil strike root. The red fruits are decorative, and the plant has merit as a ground cover.

Other tall growing species of *Euonymus* are *E. latifolia,* Zone V, and *E. sanguinea,* Zone V. Both bear red fruit, and their leaves turn red in the fall.

Exochorda Racemosa (*E. grandiflora*), Zone IV, Pearl-bush, is a native of China. It is popular in many gardens from Massachusetts southward. Slender and open in its habit, it reaches a height of fifteen feet. In late May or early June it bears racemes of pure white flowers. Pearlbush forms a splendid background shrub where lower-growing material hides its rather loose, straggly growth.

A sunny location and well-drained, slightly moist soil provide the ideal growing conditions; however, it is not an exacting plant and will succeed in almost any well-drained ground. Annual pruning after bloom is a necessity to keep the shrub as compact as possible. The best means of propagation is by layers; it can also be increased by greenwood cuttings rooted under glass.

E. Giraldii Wilsonii, Zone V, is superior to *E. racemosa;* the flowers are larger and the plant is a stronger grower.

Forsythia, Golden-bell, is one of the best-known of all flowering shrubs, and it is justly deserving of the popularity it has won. The cheerful yellow bells which clothe the bare branches in March or early April bring the message that spring is really here. *Forsythia* grows eight or nine feet high and the foliage retains its green color until late fall. It is remarkably free from insects and diseases. The upright kinds are excellent for specimens and shrub borders. The pendulous form, *F. suspensa,* falls gracefully over walls and rocky banks; it is also attractive espaliered on a fence or around a window or doorway.

Forsythia thrives in almost any soil, but it does not always bloom well in very rich ground. It can be planted in light shade, but the flowers will be more prolific in sunny locations. In the severe winters in the North the flower buds are sometimes injured.

Pruning *Forsythia* is an important part of its culture. This is done immediately after bloom. Avoid the sheared, rounded effect all too often seen, which mars the natural grace of its arching branches. Old canes should be cut out at ground level; any straggly branches should be tipped back and pruned to different lengths to conform to the plant's habit of irregularity. Unless this shrub is pruned regularly, it becomes full of dead wood and old branches that do not produce fine flowers.

Propagation is easily accomplished by layers or by cuttings of the greenwood taken during the summer and rooted in a cold frame. Cuttings can also be made from ripe wood taken in the fall. The tips of the

The bend of the walk is softened with a low planting. *Photographer, Gottscho-Schleisner.*

pendulous *F. suspensa* will strike root if they are pegged down into the ground and covered with soil.

F. intermedia, Zone IV, is a cross between the *viridissima* and the *suspensa.* It is the best species in habit of growth and combines the good qualities of both its parents. Named varieties listed by nurserymen far surpass the parent type in size, color, and profusion of bloom. *F. intermedia var. nana* is a hardy, low-growing form. *F. intermedia spectabilis* is spectacular when in bloom.

F. suspensa, Zone V, is a weeping species that grows to eight feet in height. The branches of its variety *Sieboldi* are even more pliable and lend themselves particularly well to espalier work.

F. viridissima, Zones (V) and VI, is not as attractive as the other species because of its stiff, upright habit of growth. It attains a height of nine feet. The dwarf variety *F. viridissima Bronxensis,* which was introduced by the New York Botanic Garden, is a valuable addition to the group. It does not usually exceed two feet; it blooms generously.

Certain varieties of *Forsythia* are worthy of special mention; Beatrix Farrand, Spring Glory, and Lynwood Gold.

Fothergilla, a native of the southern Appalachian Mountains, is a member of the Witch Hazel Family. It thrives in moist, peaty, light soil; it will grow in the partial shade. This bush is a little difficult to transplant; it should be moved with a good ball of earth. Propagation can be accomplished by layers and by seeds but it is a slow process. *Fothergilla* is most attractive in the blooming period and in the fall when the leaves turn brilliant red or yellow.

F. Gardeni, Zone V, is an attractive shrub three feet in height. It is useful for foundation plantings or wherever a lower-growing shrub is required in the planting scheme. It is hardy in the North; its showy flower spikes come into bloom before the leaves appear.

F. major, Zone V, is the kind most generally planted; its white flower spikes that appear in April or May are quite striking in appearance. This bush grows about eight to nine feet tall. It is densely clothed with foliage.

F. monticola, Zone V, is a handsome species six feet high, which is similar in bloom to *F. major.* It can be increased by air-layers.

Franklinia Alatamaha, Zone (V), (Gordonia), Franklin Tree, produces large white flowers that measure about three inches across; these come into bloom in September and continue to flower into October when blooms are at a premium. Its habit of growth is rather open; the foliage is glossy and turns scarlet to yellow in the fall. In cold regions it requires a sheltered position and some winter protection. North of New York it remains a shrub eight to ten feet high; whereas in the South it becomes a tree, often twenty feet tall. In home ground plantings the Franklin Tree has its place as a specimen bush on sunny lawns. A moist, sandy, peaty soil suits it best. Spring planting is preferable and must be done with care. It can be propagated by air-layers and by softwood cuttings rooted under glass.

John Bartram discovered this plant growing wild in the wooded sections of Georgia; it was named Franklin Tree in honor of his friend Benjamin Franklin. Later it was seen by John Bartram's son, and that marked the last time it was found growing in its native habitat. It is an interesting fact that all the plants in cultivation today are descendants of the original plants brought by John Bartram to his Philadelphia garden in the eighteenth century.

Gaylussacia, Huckleberry, is closely related to the Blueberry (*Vaccinium*), and its cultural requirements are similar. Both plants require acid, sandy soil with a high content of peat moss or oak leaf mold. The different kinds of Huckleberries are useful plants for naturalizing in wooded, shady locations. Propagation is best done by layering or by root cuttings.

G. baccata, Zone II, Black Huckleberry, differs from the other species in that it grows well in dry, sandy soil, and in a sunny situation. It is erect in its habit and grows about three feet tall. The sweet, black fruit is borne in August.

G. dumosa, Zone II?, Dwarf Huckleberry, is the handsomest species when in bloom, producing its white, pink, or red bells in loose racemes in May and June; these are followed by blue-black berries in midsummer. This shrub inhabits swampy, sandy ground and grows from one to two feet high.

Genista includes a group of low-growing, yellow-flowering (rarely white) plants of many species distributed through various parts of Europe, Africa, and Asia. They are deciduous or semi-evergreen. Many of the *Genistas* are well suited to the climatic conditions of California and the South.

Genista thrives in almost any soil, provided it is well-drained. A sunny location is a requisite. It is a splendid little shrub for covering rocky slopes, dry, sandy banks, rock gardens, and the forefront of shrubbery borders. The plants can be increased by seeds, layers, and cuttings of the growing wood rooted under glass.

G. germanica, Zone V, grows to about two feet; the bushes are covered with bright yellow flowers in June and July. Zero temperatures cause no trouble, provided the plant is given the congenial conditions of dry, rocky ground.

G. hispanica, Zone VI, Spanish Gorse, blooms in early June; the shrubs grow about one foot high. The twigs remain green all winter, and it is a very floriferous type. It is not reliably hardy in regions where the temperature falls to zero.

G. tinctoria, Zone II, Dyer's Greenweed, is a species that none can equal for hardiness; in June the two-foot bushes are a mass of bright yellow flowers. This plant was brought to this country by the early settlers and was later found in a Salem garden; it spread rapidly and became a troublesome weed in parts of the country. The variety *G. tinctoria plena* is a double-flowered form, and *G. tinctoria prostrata* is a dwarf type.

Other low-growing species which are sufficiently hardy to withstand temperatures at zero or below are *G. pilosa,* Zone V, a procumbent type with stems that take root as they spread; *G. radiata,* Zone (V), two to two and a half feet in height; and *G. sagittalis,* Zone IV, eight to ten inches high; its yellow flowers appear in June.

Gordonia (See Franklinia).

Halesia Carolina, Zone IV, Silverbell Tree, is an attractive shrub or small tree that has an open habit of growth and charming white bell-shaped flowers that are borne profusely in the early spring. Included in the background planting or as a lawn specimen, it gives a light, airy effect. It grows happily in almost any well-drained soil but shows a preference for a rich one. In a location where it is shielded from the high winds of winter it gives the best results. This plant is not troubled with pests, and it is long-lived.

In the North Halesia grows about fifteen feet high; however, in climates that are especially favorable it becomes tree-like in habit. Since this bush can be increased by air-layers, it is not difficult to propagate. Other methods are by seeds sown in the fall and by root cuttings.

Rose of Sharon bushes give height to the corners of the house. Yews accent the steps, and provide a dominant note to this colorful dooryard garden. *Photographer, Paul E. Genereux.*

Hamamelis, Witch-Hazel, produces yellow flowers that brighten the woodlands at a time of year when color is most appreciated. For this reason it has its definite use in the planting scheme. The native kinds are preeminently plants for informal, shady, wooded places, where their welcome blooms are silhouetted against the evergreens and the bare branches of the deciduous trees.

Witch-Hazel prefers a soil that is moist and that contains a fair amount of sand and peat. The Chinese species likes more sun and less moisture than the native kinds; it is more showy in flower than the American forms. Branches of the winter and spring flowering types can be brought into the house almost any time during the cold winter months and forced into bloom.

H. mollis, Zone V, Chinese Witch-Hazel, is a superior species because of its larger flowers and better habit of growth. The delightfully fragrant blooms unfold at any time from January to March, depending upon weather conditions. It can reach a height of thirty feet; however, it responds well to pruning and can be kept within bounds. The foliage turns yellow in the autumn.

H. vernalis, Zone V, is a native species that rarely exceeds eight feet. The flowering period is variable, and it comes into bloom any time in January, February, or March. A warm spell in midwinter frequently induces the yellow flowers to burst into bloom.

H. virginiana, Zone IV, is another native floriferous Witch-Hazel that abounds in wooded margins and swamp borders from Canada to Florida. It is a shrub or small tree fifteen feet in height. This bush is of special interest because of its late blooming period, which usually commences in October and extends into November. In the fall the leaves turn a clear yellow. Undoubtedly it was this shrub that John G. Whittier had in mind when he wrote the following lines:

> *Through the gray and sombre wood,*
> *Against the dusk of fir and pine,*
> *Last of their floral sisterhood,*
> *The hazel's yellow blossoms shine.*

Hibiscus Syriacus, Zone (V), Althaea, Rose of Sharon, is an old-fashioned favorite that was brought to this country in the days of the early settlers. It is well suited for hedges or as an enclosure to simple flower gardens on country places which are designed along informal lines. It also has a definite use in suburban gardens, where it can be worked in as a specimen or in the foundation planting. It will also tolerate the conditions of city yards. Its stiff, upright habit makes it rather difficult to combine in a mixed shrubbery planting; however, it can be successfully tied in as a background shrub where bushes of more graceful lines soften the effect. The chief assets of Rose of Sharon are the large size of its blooms and its midsummer flowering period, which arrives in all its freshness when the blooms of most shrubs have come and gone.

Varieties of Rose of Sharon are obtainable in white, pink, red, lilac, clear pink, and bluish-purple; the best ones to select are the white and clear pink.

This shrub likes soil that is not too dry and a situation that is sunny; it will stand some light shade. Aphids are frequently troublesome, but they can be eradicated with repeated sprayings of nicotine. Althaea can be increased by air layers, seeds, and cuttings.

Hippophae Rhamnoides, Zone III, Sea-Buckthorn, is a hardy, upright shrub or small tree, usually fifteen feet tall but occasionally attaining a height of thirty feet. This shrub is principally grown for the autumn effect of its orange fruit, which persists on the branches into the winter. However, for berry production a male plant must be included in the planting.

Sea-Buckthorn is a good plant for seashore gardens, where it grows in poor, sandy soil. Propagation is by air-layers, suckers, seeds, and cuttings.

Hydrangea is a hardy plant that is grown chiefly for the large, handsome panicles of white blooms which appear in midsummer. The flowering period is an extensive one, and in the fall the blooms change from white to a dull rose or reddish color. The flowers can be cut for indoor decoration and will remain in good condition into the winter.

Hydrangeas are often overworked in foundation plantings. If they are planted sparingly, they can give pleasing results. A specimen of *Hydrangea* in full bloom gives a striking effect. These shrubs are among the most useful ones for seashore gardens and grow luxuriantly in the moist atmosphere which prevails in such localities. They thrive best in soils that are rich and moist and in situations that are either sunny or partially shady. When given the full sun the flowers will be more abundant, especially if the plants are not allowed to suffer from drought. In dry weather copious watering is an essential.

Most *Hydrangeas* are pruned early in spring before growth commences. All weak and dead wood should be removed, and the lateral shoots cut back to two to three buds from the main stems; the severity of the trimming will depend upon the number and the size of the flowers desired. Lighter pruning than that mentioned above will give a greater number of blooms at the expense of size. *H. quercifolia* and *H. macrophylla Hortensia* are exceptions to the rule as to the time to prune; both species are cut back immediately after bloom. The trimming consists of cutting out the old branches and shortening back those that are retained. The propagation of *Hydrangeas* is by suckers, layers, or by cuttings taken in summer and rooted in a shaded frame. *H. quercifolia* is best increased by layers or by suckers.

H. arborescens grandiflora, Hills-of-Snow, is a hardy, undemanding shrub usually three—but sometimes ten—feet tall. It is an old-time garden habitué, seen most generally on farms and in old-fashioned gardens. The white flowers appear in July. Some growers recommend cutting back the plant close to ground level in earliest spring.

H. macrophylla Hortensia, Greenhouse Hydrangea, often referred to as "French Hydrangea," is not reliably hardy where the winters are severe. In the cold regions it is grown as a tub plant for patio decoration in summer. During the winter it is kept in a frost-proof place or wintered outdoors with substantial protection. It is the Hydrangea most frequently seen in seashore gardens along the New Jersey coast and southward. In mild climates this plant is a real favorite, and it is grown outdoors extensively. It also grows well in city yards. An interesting characteristic of this plant is the fact that the color of the blue varieties will turn pink if the soil becomes alkaline. An acid soil is required to maintain the blue color. To provide acidity, plants grown in tubs are watered with alum, using one teaspoonful of alum to one gallon of water. When grown outdoors, peat moss or acid leaf mold and sand incorporated into the ground will help retain the blue color. A good pink flowering variety is *rosea*.

H. paniculata grandiflora, Peegee Hydrangea, is one of the hardiest species; unless it is kept within bounds by pruning, it can grow into a tree twenty-five feet in height. It is widely planted and is valued for its large white flower clusters which bloom in August. It is suitable only for use as a specimen.

H. quercifolia, Zone (V), Oak Leaf Hydrangea, is a southern species with distinctive leaves that resemble those of a red oak tree. In the North the bloom is uncertain, since the bush is apt to winter-kill to the ground. A location in the partial shade is preferable, especially in warm climates. Pruning should not be done until after bloom.

H. Sargentiana, Zone VII?, Sargent Hydrangea, is not reliably hardy north of Delaware; however, in genial climates it is a lovely shrub with large, flat flower clusters that appear in July or August. The combination of the blue-violet fertile flowers with the surrounding white sterile flowers is unusual and decorative. This *Hydrangea* does best if it is planted in the partial shade; its height is approximately nine feet.

Hypericum, St. John's-wort, is a lovely low-growing plant with gay yellow flowers which brighten the midsummer garden. This shrub prefers a light, sandy, well-drained soil; it will grow in sun or partial shade. The taller kinds are attractive as facers to the shrubbery border; the more dwarf species lend themselves admirably for use in rock gardens, for edging purposes, or as ground covers. The supply can be increased by seeds; the creeping kinds are propagated by suckers and division.

H. Buckleyi, Zone V, makes a good ground cover less than one foot high. Its blooming season is the middle of June.

H. calycinum, Zone (V), Aaron's-beard, is desirable as a ground cover or for adding color to the rock garden in July. It grows well in the partial shade. This plant is easily increased by means of suckers. It is semi-evergreen or evergreen.

H. Kalmianum, Zone IV, Kalm St. John's-wort, is three feet tall and has evergreen leaves. The effective flowers bloom in July.

H. Moserianum, Zone VII?, Gold-flower, is an exceptionally charming plant, with flowers that measure two and a half inches across; the bloom commences in July and contributes its golden beauty to the garden for a protracted period. Its slender, graceful branches grow to two feet in height.

H. patulum Henryi, Zone (V), VI, is one of the most desirable species. In the North it should be given winter protection. It grows three feet tall. This species also has a long season of bloom which begins in late July.

H. prolificum, Zone IV, is a hardy, compact shrub four feet high. The flowers appear in July and continue to bloom for quite an extended period.

Chapter XIII

Flowering Shrubs—I through M

Indigofera Kirilowii, Zone IV, a native of China, is an attractive shrub three or four feet tall. It is an excellent bush for shrubbery borders, where its spikes of small rose-pink flowers appear in June and July. It thrives in well-drained soils that contain peat moss or leaf mold. Propagation is of the simplest, since the shrub spreads rapidly and can be increased by suckers. *I. amblyantha,* Zone V, has a long-blooming period; its lilac to purple flower spikes appear in late May or early June.

Itea Virginica, Zone V, Virginia Willow, Sweetspire, is of special use for problem spots, such as damp ground and shady locations, but it will also adapt itself to sunny situations and to practically any kind of garden soil. It grows to a height of eight feet; the fragrant white flowers are produced in June or July. The foliage takes on red autumnal tints. Plants can be increased by seed, cuttings, or root divisions.

Jamesia Americana, Zone IV, is an interesting hardy shrub indigenous to the Rocky Mountain region. It grows to about four feet. This bush is good for introducing variety in the planting scheme. It likes a sunny location and will grow in most well-drained soils. However, it prefers those that are light and that contain acid organic matter. Propagation is by seeds and cuttings of the ripe wood.

Jasminum Nudiflora, Zone (V), Jasmine, is one of those welcome early-comers that brings the promise of brighter days to come. Its cheerful, fragrant, yellow flowers often open during mild spells in late winter. Trained around a window or doorway, or espaliered on a wall, Jasmine

189

Before landscaping, this house was considered one of the ugliest in the community.

appears at its best; planted on the top of a bank the pliable branches fall gracefully over it, clothing it with a shower of golden blooms. When it is grown as a bush, it is apt to turn into a tangled, straggly mass unless it is pruned regularly. Jasmine attains a height of eight feet; it is hardy as far north as southern New York State. It thrives in fertile garden soil. This plant is readily propagated by cuttings and by layers.

Kerria Japonica, Zone IV, Kerria, is a widely grown shrub that is valued for its ornamental bright yellow flowers which are produced abundantly in May or early June. It grows to about six feet, but it can be kept considerably lower by pruning. It is excellent for the shrubbery border and for foundation planting. The numerous slender branches retain their green color throughout the winter.

To lower the awkward height of the house the foundation of the sun porch was retained to form a raised planting bed. The iron rail by the steps and the attractive corner planting of shrubbery combine to give this house a new look. *Owner, Mrs. Gideon Boericke. Landscape Architect, Frances V. Finletter. Courtesy Horticulture. Photographer, the Roches.*

These two pictures show the desolation before the
property was landscaped.

This patio was created by removing the back wall of the service room. The window frames were taken out to give light and air to the patio. The ceiling and walls were plastered. A flagstone flooring and potted plants on the window sills decorate this living area which overlooks the secluded garden. *Owner, Mrs Gideon Boericke. Landscape Architect, Frances V. Finletter. Photographer, the Roches.*

Kerria grows in almost any well-drained soil; it prefers light shade, although it will do satisfactorily in full sun. Because of its spreading habit of growth, a rather severe annual pruning is required to keep the plant within bounds; this should be done after the blooming period. It can easily be increased by division or by layers; it can also be propagated by cuttings taken from the growing wood and rooted in a shaded frame. *K. j. pleniflora,* Japanese Rose, Globe Flower, is a double-flowered form which is even more popular than the single kind. It is taller and more vigorous.

Kolkwitzia Amabilis, Zone V, Beauty-bush, is well named. It is one of the loveliest bushes among the flowering shrubs. It should certainly be one of the choices for a planting scheme in which there is sufficient room for a bush of generous proportions. The delicate, bell-shaped flowers appear in May or early June in shades of soft pink and literally cover the bush with their beauty; they are rather similar to the blooms of *Weigela,*

The bleak backyard was turned into a livable, secluded garden adjoining the patio. Shrubs along the fence and flowers in the foreground
complete this simple, effective lay-out. *Owner, Mrs. Gideon Boericke.*
Landscape Architect, Frances V. Finletter. Courtesy Horticulture. Pho-
tographer, the Roches.

but they are smaller in size; in fact, the shrubs are related. The small leaves are in keeping with the dainty flowers and give a good effect at all times. This garden treasure came to us from China; it is a member of the Honeysuckle Family.

When you plant a young bush, do not be surprised if it fails to bloom. It will not start to flower until it takes root and becomes thoroughly at home in its new quarters. The best bloom can be obtained by growing *Kolkwitzia* in poor ground; it demands a place in the full sun; otherwise the flower effect will be disappointing. If grown under congenial conditions, it becomes a broad shrub nine or ten feet high. When planted as a specimen, its aesthetic value is seen at its best, where the arching branches fall in graceful lines. The best means of propagation is by cuttings taken from the growing wood late in summer.

Laburnum, Golden-chain, is one of the outstanding small trees for garden effect, growing to twenty or thirty feet in height. In late May or early June it bears graceful, drooping racemes of Wisteria-like yellow flowers, which contrast effectively with the dark green tri-foliate leaves. It is not fastidious as to soil. It will grow in any well-drained ground, although it seems to prefer soil that contains some lime. It will thrive in sun or partial shade. This plant can be increased by layers and seeds; the finer kinds are multiplied by grafting and budding.

L. anagyroides, Zone (V), is the Common Laburnum which attains a height of about twenty feet. It does not tolerate the extreme cold of northern winters. Unfortunately it is frequently destroyed by borers. Some of its most desirable forms are *autumnale* (which blooms again late in the summer), *bullatum* (curled leaves), *aureum* (yellow foliage), *quercifolium* (leaves are lobed), and *pendulum* (branches are drooping).

L. alpinum, Zone IV, Scotch Laburnum, has a misleading common name, for it actually comes from southern Europe. This species tolerates the cold temperatures of Massachusetts. Its blooming season is two weeks later than *L. anagyroides;* it is stiffer and more upright in its habit, and the flower racemes are longer and thinner.

L. watereri, Zone V (*L. Vossi*), when in full bloom, is transformed into a shower of golden, pendulous flowers. It is charming for softening the corner of the house or wall, or in the garden where the line of planting needs to be broken with a tall growing specimen. This variety is a noteworthy hybrid of *L. anagyroides* and *L. alpinum*. It is a light-growing, small tree, well adapted to the average home grounds.

Lagerstroemia Indica, Zone VII, Crape-Myrtle, is an intriguing shrub that grows to twenty or twenty-one feet in height. It is available in several varieties, the flower panicles appearing in white, pink, purplish-red, and purple. It comes to our gardens from China. This bush is among the favorite flowering shrubs and is quite generally grown in this country where milder temperatures prevail, especially in the South. It is not reliably hardy north of Baltimore, but it can be grown in the area of Philadelphia provided it is planted in a somewhat protected location. In regions where the cold is more severe, Crape-Myrtle can be enjoyed if given tub or pot culture and grown in a cool greenhouse. It will come into flower several times if it is pruned drastically.

Not only is Crape-Myrtle a free-flowering plant, but it also blooms a number of months in the summer. The flowers are crinkly and large, many of them measuring about one and a half inches across. In some parts of the country it is used as hedge material. It is always lovely when grown as a specimen, and it works in well among the tall-growing background shrubs.

L. indica var. nana is a dwarf form; the violet flowers are very effective throughout the summer. It is attractive in the front part of the shrubbery border, as well as in various spots where a lower-growing plant is required. The variety *prostrata* is prostrate in its habit; it produces pink blossoms.

It is very simple to start new plants from seed, and they will bear flowers the first season after seeding; the supply can also be increased by cuttings made from the ripe wood. It responds well to pruning, which makes the bush more compact. The foliage turns yellow and crimson before it falls. This plant is not easy to move; it should be transplanted with a good ball of earth around the roots.

Unfortunately Crape-Myrtle sometimes falls prey to mildew, a particularly bad pest in the California coast area. This white powdery disease affects the leaves and the shoots. It can be controlled with one spraying of commercial Lime-sulphur, using one part to eighty parts of water; it should be applied when the buds begin to open in the spring. If any further spraying is needed, Mildex is excellent for the purpose, but this should not be used unless the temperature is below eighty degrees. Aphids are another pest, sometimes so severe that they cause the leaves to fall; a contact insecticide, such as Nicotine-sulphate, will combat the infesta-

A formally clipped hedge encloses a portion of lawn area, turning it into a turf terrace. Simplicity of design has been stressed. *Photographer, Paul E. Genereux.*

tion. The honeydew that these insects exude provides a good medium in which the sooty-mold fungus flourishes; it is recognized by the foliage becoming blackened; the same treatment that is given for aphids will also take care of this pest.

Ligustrum, Privet, comes in deciduous and evergreen forms (see page 103) and in innumerable species. The flowers appear in white spikes; the fruit is blue-black or black, and it usually persists on the branches through the winter. This is one of the most adaptable shrubs available; it is not fastidious as to soil requirements, it grows in sun or shade (preferably in sun); and it succeeds well in city yards and seashore gardens. Its uses are well known: for hedges, screening, foundation plantings. Certain kinds also lend themselves to topiary work, for example *L. ovalifolium* (California Privet). Some of the Privets winter-kill badly in the North, but if they are pruned back drastically, new shoots soon replace the loss; in fact, when bushier plants are required, a good pruning will give the needed results. The plants are increased by seed and by cuttings. Grafting is employed to propagate especially desirable kinds; the stock used to graft on is *L. ovalifolium* or *L. vulgare*.

L. acuminatum, Zone IV, comes from Japan. It grows six feet high, and the top-growth is rather spreading in habit. This species loses its foliage early in the autumn. Its black berries are shiny. The leaves of its variety *macrocarpum* are larger, and the bush is a more upright grower.

L. amurense, Zone III, Amur Privet, is a Chinese species; it retains its light-green foliage late in the season. Being especially hardy, it is useful in the North for hedges. It attains a height of fifteen feet.

L. Henryi, Zone VII, Henry Privet, grows to about twelve feet; in the autumn the black berries are attractive.

L. ibolium, Zone V, is not as hardy as the Amur Privet, but it has a better habit of growth.

L. obtusifolium, Zone III, Border Privet, is one of the hardiest types. It bears a generous crop of black berries. The variety *Regelianum*, Zone V, Regel Privet, is widely planted; it does not grow more than four or five feet high, which makes it good for foundation plantings. To increase the supply it is best to grow it from cuttings rather than from seeds in order to ensure reproducing the original shape of the shrub. The blue-black berries persist until the leaves begin to unfold in spring.

L. ovalifolium, Zone (V), California Privet, is semi-evergreen. It attains a height of fifteen feet. This species is not as hardy as various other kinds, and in temperatures below zero it dies back to the ground. The shiny leaves add to its popularity. This shrub is somewhat stiff in appearance. In localities where the winters are severe, the black berries do not usually appear. The variety *aureo-marginatum*, Golden Privet, is even less hardy; a sunny situation and good garden soil are required for best results. The variety *nanum* is a dwarf form.

L. Quihoui, Zone VI, is of Chinese origin. It is a medium-size shrub, growing six feet tall. If it is planted in the North, it should not be placed in an exposed location, and it should be given a light soil. Its spreading branches are rather stiff. In midsummer its long flower spikes are very effective.

L. sinense, Zone VII, Chinese Privet, is a handsome shrub. It is another species that produces very attractive large panicles of flowers in summer.

It is not hardy in climates where the winters are cold. This shrub grows twelve feet high.

L. vulgare, Zone IV, Common Privet, is deciduous or semi-evergreen; it retains its green leaves a long time. This European plant grows fifteen feet tall. The flower panicles are followed by shiny black berries. It appears in various forms; the variety *Xanthocarpum* bears yellow fruit. *L. vulgare var. Lodense* is a dwarf kind.

Lindera Benzoin, Zone IV, Spice-bush, is so-called because of the fragrance of its leaves, fruit, and branches. It is found growing in damp, wooded locations from New England southward and west to Kansas. The clusters of pale-yellow flowers open in late April before the shrub is in leaf. Spice-bush is a broad, tall shrub six to fifteen feet high. Its crimson berries and the bright yellow tints of its foliage in fall add to the autumn landscape. This plant is appropriate for use along the banks of streams, and in swampy ground—in fact, it is of value in any informal surroundings.

Spice-bush is a hardy plant and is relatively free from insects and diseases. Although a sandy, moist soil that is supplied with peat moss or leaf mold suits it best, it will also grow satisfactorily in any average garden soil in a shady location. Propagation is by seeds, and greenwood cuttings rooted under glass. The seeds must be sown when they ripen because they soon lose their vitality.

At the time of the Revolutionary War the dried, pulverized berries are said to have been used for allspice, and in the days of the Civil War the leaves were used for tea.

Lonicera, Honeysuckle, appears in different forms that vary in their habit of growth from vines to shrubs, and from deciduous to evergreen types. This genus for the most part is hardy in the North. Most of the species like a sunny situation, although certain kinds will tolerate partial shade. In order to develop the maximum number of flowers and berries, full sun is required. Honeysuckle is much loved for the deliciously fragrant blooms of many of the species. Some of the bushes produce attractive showy berries. Honeysuckle grows happily in practically any soil, provided it is not wet. It will thrive with no special care, and it responds well to pruning. It can be increased from seeds, layers, and cuttings of the ripened wood.

The solid green hedge serves as a background for shrubbery and perennials. *Photographer, Paul E. Genereux.*

The landscape uses for the bush forms are as screens and in shrubbery borders, and the best types can be planted as specimens.

L. alpigena, Zone V, is of European origin; it grows eight feet tall. The coloring of the flowers is especially lovely, appearing in a yellowish shade touched with red. Late in the summer the scarlet berries are very effective. The variety *nana* is a dwarf grower three feet high. The dark-red flowers that open in May are not effective, but the red fruit is attractive in fall.

L. amoena arnoldiana, Arnold Honeysuckle, produces rather large pale pink blooms about the middle of May; these, together with the graceful habit of growth, make it suitable for specimen planting, as well as for the shrubbery border and for screening purposes. It attains a height of nine feet.

L. chrysantha, Zone III, is a very hardy, upright-growing shrub reaching twelve feet in height. It bears creamy-white to yellow blooms, and it produces a wealth of red berries.

L. fragrantissima, Zone (V), Winter Honeysuckle, is a semi-evergreen that grows eight feet high. The creamy-white flowers bring their lovely fragrance to the garden early in the spring; in addition to its early blooming habit that is always welcome, it is among the first bushes to come into fruit.

L. gracilipes, Zone V, Spangle Honeysuckle, is another early bloomer. Its flowers open in shades of pink to carmine, on attractively arching branches. In June the red fruit adds color to the planting. This shrub grows six feet high.

L. Korolkowii, Zone IV, Blue-leaf Honeysuckle, bursts into bloom late in May; the pale pink flowers blend well with the bluish-green foliage. It grows to generous proportions, reaching a height of twelve feet. This shrub is not easy to transplant. It produces scarlet to deep yellow berries in late summer.

L. Ledebourii, Zone (V), Ledebour Honeysuckle, is native to California; it has dark-green leaves that set off the lovely deep yellow blooms that are touched with scarlet. The black berries are ornamental in summer. This shrub attains a height of fifteen feet.

L. Maackii, Zone II, Amur Honeysuckle, is a very hardy, strong-growing shrub about fifteen feet tall. The foliage is a rich green shade, and the flowers are rather large and conspicuous. They are white (turning to yellowish) and sweetly fragrant, and they bloom toward the end of May, being late for the Honeysuckles. The red fruit is quite showy in fall, which is one of the strong points of the Amur strain, and the berries persist sometimes until late November. The variety *podocarpa,* Zone IV, is more spreading in habit; it comes into bloom in June.

L. microphylla, Zone V, is a dwarf Honeysuckle three feet in height; its flowers that bloom in May are fragrant and yellowish-white. This species can stand temperatures below zero.

L. Morrowii, Zone III, Morrow Honeysuckle, is indigenous to Japan. Its habit of growth is very spreading, and it attains a height of eight feet. The flowers are white, changing to yellow, and they appear near the end of May. It bears dark-red berries that are relished by the birds.

L. prostrata, Zone V, is a Chinese species which forms thick mats or a

Spring has really come when *Magnolia stellata* bursts into bloom. Used as a specimen this shrub appears at its best. *Photographer, the Roches.*

low shrub. The white flowers have no value, but the bright red fruit is gay. Its hardiness cannot be counted upon in temperatures below zero.

L. spinosa var. Alberti, Zone III, is a low-growing, graceful, and very hardy shrub. Its fragrant pink flowers open in June.

L. syringantha, Zone IV, Lilac Honeysuckle, is a dense-growing shrub six to nine feet high. The branches are partly prostrate, and the leaves are rather small. The fragrant flowers are somewhat similar to those of the lilac, and they come in blush-white to pinkish-lavender. Under favorable conditions the shrub is very free-flowering. The scarlet fruit is decorative in June. The variety *Wolfii* bears fragrant, carmine blooms, and the leaves are narrower than the type.

L. tatarica, Zone IV, Tatarian Honeysuckle, is one of the finest among the bush Honeysuckles; it is a variable species. It thrives in almost any soil. The flowers give a dainty effect and are produced abundantly in either pink or white. The dark-red berries are very effective and are loved by the birds. The variety *lutea* has yellow fruit, and the variety *parviflora* produces orange-red berries; its flowers are small and white in color. Some of the best varieties are: *rosea,* whose rosy-pink flowers are lighter in shade on the inner side; *sibirica,* with deep pink blooms; *latifolia,* also pink-flowering, with large flowers and leaves; *alba,* a white-flowering form; and *angustifolia,* with light pink blooms. The variety *nana* is a dwarf-growing form with a generous number of small pinkish flowers.

L. thibetica, Zone IV, has a spreading habit, reaching about four feet in height. The foliage is a rich green, and the upper surface of the leaves is glossy. It produces fragrant, pale-purple flowers the middle of May. The red berries are decorative and appear in early summer. It is well adapted for planting on rocky slopes.

Magnolia Stellata, Zone V, Star Magnolia, is the earliest Magnolia to bloom after the cold winter months; in fact, in the North the beautiful pure white double flowers that appear before the leaves are frequently caught by late frosts. In such latitudes it is best to plant it in a northern exposure to discourage its bursting into bloom quite so early. The flowers measure about three inches or more across; they bloom profusely and are delightfully fragrant. One of the greatest thrills in the arrival of spring is to watch for these lovely flowers to open their petals.

M. stellata is the hardiest type among the Magnolias. This shrub or small tree has a dense habit of growth. In this country it is usually twelve to fifteen feet tall, but it attains a much greater height in its native Japan. The usual methods of propagation are by seeds, layers, and cuttings taken from the green wood. This plant prefers a fertile soil that contains some moisture; it is well to incorporate leaf mold or peat moss and sand in the soil when it is planted. *M. stellata* does not transplant easily; it should be moved with a ball of earth around the roots. The large fleshy roots decay rapidly when bruised or broken, and they are not likely to recover if transplanted when the growth is not active; consequently this should be done in early spring, either when the shrub is in bloom or when the leaves just begin to unfold. It likes a sunny exposure.

In fall the Star Magnolia adds to the autumn coloring with its red fruit and with the leaves that turn yellow and bronzy. The variety *Water Lily* has more double blooms than the type, and the variety *rosea* is pink in bud, the flowers later turning to white.

You could not choose a lovelier specimen than *Magnolia stellata* for the entrance to the drive, for the lawn, or wherever a shrub is needed to stand alone in all its beauty.

Myrica Pensylvanica, Zone II, (*M. caroliniensis*), Bayberry, is found in its native habitat from Nova Scotia to Florida and westward. It grows principally along the seashore, where it thrives in the sandy soil. This shrub is semi-evergreen and grows to a height of nine feet. The decorative leaves are aromatic, and it produces attractive waxy, gray berries from which the candles are made. The staminate and pistillate flowers are not on the same plant; consequently bushes of each sex should be placed near each other for good berry production. The propagation is by seeds, suckers, and layers.

Chapter XIV

Flowering Shrubs—N through Sy

Nandina Domestica, Zone VII?, Heavenly Bamboo, a native of China and Japan, is a shrub with great appeal. The soft effect of its foliage is unusually attractive. In the South this shrub is evergreen, but where the winters are severe it is deciduous and does not leaf-out until quite late in spring. *Nandina* is generally considered to be a mild climate plant, but it is certainly worth while for gardeners in the Philadelphia area to experiment with its culture. In cold winters the bush may winter-kill to the ground, but new shoots will spring up when the weather becomes warm; it has been known to stand temperatures around zero or below. When the leaves first appear in spring, they are delicately tinted light-red, changing to soft lush green as they develop. The terminal white flower clusters begin to bloom in July, and these are followed by bright red berries. The birds pass these by, so that the bushes are not robbed of their fruit, and this combined with the red autumnal foliage makes Nandina a gaily colored fall shrub.

A light, moist soil that is well supplied with oak leaf mold or peat moss will provide the most congenial conditions. A year-round mulch of compost, leaf mold, or peat moss will also help the growth. A situation in partial shade is preferable; however, it will grow in full sun. An early spring feeding applied before growth starts will be beneficial; this can be repeated in late spring. Dry weather during the blooming season often

205

prevents the setting of the fruit; consequently watering at that time will help to assure the fall crop of berries. Heavenly Bamboo is free from insect pests and diseases. Propagation is by seeds and by cuttings; occasionally a shoot may appear on the side of the bush, which can be severed from the parent plant with the roots intact.

Neillia Sinensis, Zone V, is a choice shrub of Asiatic origin, and it should be better known. It grows to about six feet; it is a graceful bush with arching branches and clear pink flowers that come in June. This is a shrub for the small place; it can be worked into the planting scheme either singly or in groupings in the mixed border. It thrives in practically any moist soil of average fertility. Propagation is not difficult; it can be grown from seeds stratified in the fall, or by cuttings of the growing wood taken during the summer and rooted under glass.

Philadelphus, Mock-Orange, is a familiar habitué of the gardens of yesterday and of today. Because of the delicious fragrance of its pure white flowers, it fully deserves the popularity it has won. The habit of growth is not particularly ornamental or distinctive, nor does the foliage provide autumnal color; therefore it must be regarded as a plant that only gives effect during its blooming period.

Mock-Orange requires little or no care other than an annual pruning after the flowering period. It does well in sun or partial shade; it is practically immune to insects and diseases. This shrub will succeed in almost any well-drained soil; however, it does best in ground that is moist and fertile. Propagation is by division and by softwood and hardwood cuttings.

P. coronarius, Zone IV, Sweet Mock-Orange, European in origin, has been cultivated in gardens for hundreds of years. It is a broad, dense shrub about ten feet high; the flowers are delightfully fragrant. This Mock-Orange is especially useful for screening and for background purposes. *P. coronarius var. duplex* bears fragrant, double flowers; it is a dwarf form, upright-growing, with slender, arching branches.

The great French hybridizer Lemoine and his successors have given us a new race of Mock-Oranges that are of the greatest value to home gardeners. This was accomplished by crossing the two fragrant species *P. coronarius* and the lower-growing southern *P. microphyllus,* Zone V. These species have imparted their delicious scent to their offspring, and

A background planting of shrubs provides an effective setting for this terrace garden. *Photographer, Paul E. Genereux.*

the varieties which have resulted are greatly superior to the parents; they grow about six feet high.

Not all Mock-Oranges are fragrant, and since this quality is the most important consideration in selecting varieties, hybrids which possess it in full measure are the most desirable. Included among the fragrant *Lemoine Hybrids,* Zone V, are such favorites as Avalanche, Mont Blanc, Belle Etoile, Boule d'Argent (a double-flowering form), Candelabra, Innocence, and Perle Blanche.

P. virginalis var. Virginal is one of the finest of this group; it has large, fragrant, double flowers. Contrary to most Mock-Oranges it produces occasional flowers throughout the season. However, the blossoms which follow the burst of June bloom are scattered and cannot be depended upon to give any real effect. This shrub has an open habit of growth, and unless it is kept judiciously pruned, the plant is apt to become straggly. Pruning is best done immediately after the flowering period in June. The exact parentage of *P. virginalis* is not definitely known, but it is thought to be the result of crossing *P. Lemoinei* with *P. nivalis.*

Physocarpus Opulifolius, Zone II, Ninebark, is a decorative shrub eight or ten feet high. It has bright green leaves, and effective, fluffy, white flower heads that bloom in late May or early June. It is hardy, vigorous, and grows rapidly. This bush is easily transplanted; it will thrive in almost any soil that is moist, will endure partial shade, and does not often become diseased. Propagation is accomplished by means of seeds and cuttings taken either of the growing wood in summer or of the mature growth in fall. When planted in masses in the background, it is very effective; it is also useful for screening purposes.

P. amurensis, Zone IV, is a species from the Amur River valley. It is a taller shrub and a more vigorous grower than *P. opulifolius;* otherwise it is similar and is used for the same purposes.

P. bracteatus, Zone V, grows to a height of six feet. It has a finer foliage effect than *P. opulifolius* and is more compact in its habit of growth. Its blooming period is in June, and the flowers are somewhat larger than those of the latter species.

P. monogynus, Zone V, is a species from the Rocky Mountains; it is a dense, spreading shrub about three feet high. The small, fluffy white flowers are pink in the center.

The dividing fence line is clothed with a mixed shrubbery planting. *Photographer, Paul E. Genereux.*

Poncirus Trifoliata, Zone (V), VI (*Citrus trifoliata*), Hardy-orange, is a distinctive shrub of Chinese origin. It grows to fifteen or twenty feet; the dense, lustrous, dark-green foliage is similar in effect to that of an evergreen. The white blossoms which appear in April are followed by conspicuous fruit that resembles small oranges. Planted close to the house or the outdoor living area, it gives a touch suggestive of the tropics. All winter long the branches retain their green color, which makes it an interesting shrub for the winter landscape. Hardy-orange is well equipped with formidable thorns, which certainly do not contribute to the pleasure of pruning! Nevertheless this should be done to keep the bush compact. It is a splendid plant for living hedges which are designed to keep intruders out of the garden.

This shrub is not reliably hardy north of New York, but it is grown successfully in sheltered locations as far north as Boston. It thrives best in an acid soil. The plant seeds itself freely in the latitude of Philadelphia. If this natural form of propagation does not occur, the seeds can be sown in boxes of moist sphagnum moss and stored through the winter indoors.

Prinsepia Sinensis, Zone IV, is also a thorny bush that is sometimes used as a living fence. It is indigenous to Manchuria. The bright green foliage appears in early spring before the majority of other shrubs are in leaf. Its yellow flower-clusters are borne in the leaf axils along the stems; they are not showy, but are followed in summer by cherry-like purple fruits. *Prinsepia* does not usually exceed six feet in height. It likes a sunny location in well-drained soil. The plant is best increased by layers. *P. uniflora,* Zone V, develops into a thick bush, and in common with *P. sinensis* it is a good barrier plant. The white flowers are followed by purple-red fruit. Since the branches are white, this shrub has some winter value.

Prunus Maritima, Zone III, Beach Plum, can be seen growing contentedly in the poor, sandy soil which prevails at the seashore, even tolerating the ocean spray. For inland gardens the Beach Plum also has its place; it can be planted under oak or pine trees, used for naturalistic plantings, or included in the shrubbery border. This shrub grows into a rounded bush about five feet high and is well clothed with vigorous, dark-green leaves. The numerous white flowers which appear in early May are followed by dull purple or red fruit, which is excellent for jams and jellies. *P. maritima flava* is a yellow-fruited form.

Propagation is by root cuttings (see page 48) and by seed. The easiest way to obtain the plants is to collect them from their native haunts. Some of the named varieties being grown by a few nurserymen are superior to the type.

Prunus Glandulosa, Zone IV, Flowering Almond, is an enchanting dwarf shrub of Chinese origin. It was widely planted in old-fashioned gardens and remains a favorite today. Its charm lies in the myriads of clear, true pink double flowers which crowd the branches in April. The difficulty with this shrub is that it is a one-season plant and lacks interest except during the blooming period. Its habit of growth is bushy, but the dull green leaves are not ornamental. It can easily be kept within bounds by pruning. Unfortunately it is subject to borers; however, on the favorable side of the picture, Flowering Almond needs no special care and thrives in ordinary soil.

The wall that retains the upper level is softened with groupings of shrubbery. *Photographer, Paul E. Genereux.*

Plants grown on their own roots are preferable to those that are grafted. Ordinarily this shrub forms a thick clump that can easily be increased by division. It is obtainable in both white and pink flowers and in single or double blooms; the double-flowering pink kind that forms little rosettes along the branches is the best type to select.

Rhodotypos Scandens, Zone IV (*R. kerrioides*), Jet-Bead, White Kerria, is not one of the best flowering shrubs but it should not be overlooked. This adaptable plant will tolerate clay soils; it will thrive in partly shady or in sunny situations. *Rhodotypos* grows about three to six feet high; the light green foliage sets off the single white flowers that are borne abundantly in May. The chief value of this shrub is its shiny, black fruits which persist on the branches all winter. The small home owner will find this to be a bush that will fit into practically any part of the planting scheme, and it is useful for city yards.

White Kerria has no special cultural requirements. It is a moderately vigorous grower and should be pruned immediately after bloom to maintain a compact growth. Propagation is by softwood cuttings taken in summer; if the plants are allowed to go to seed, they will probably increase themselves naturally.

Rhus Coggygria (*Cotinus Coggygria*), Zone V, Smoke-tree, is an unusual and interesting shrub that is believed to have been a garden inhabitant for two thousand years. Ordinarily it does not exceed six feet, but it can grow to fifteen feet in height. The principal ornamental value of the Smoke-tree is its large, feathery panicles of bloom that crown the tips of the branches in June or July. The color of these panicles is an unusual shade of dull rose or mauve, and they give to the shrub the appearance of a dense cloud of smoke. This "smoke" is a curious plumose development which follows the flowering.

Smoke-tree is one of those satisfactory shrubs that can be planted where the soil conditions are rather dry and poor—in fact, all it asks is a sunny location in well-drained ground for its home. It is not too easy to transplant; but when it is once established, it will flourish with little or no care. The variety *purpureus* has purple flower panicles, and its leaves also have a purplish hue. In the fall the foliage of both species turns a brilliant yellow. Propagation is best accomplished by layers and by root cuttings.

Robinia Hispida, Zone V, Rose-Acacia, is an arresting shrub when in bloom; the pendulous clusters of rose-pink flowers resemble those of wisteria. Its blooming period is in June; the gay blossoms add their touch of beauty to that colorful month. Rose-Acacia grows to a height of about three feet and the finely divided foliage is ornamental. Its uses are rather limited because of its straggly habit of growth and its inclination to travel by means of suckers; it must either be given plenty of space in which to grow or else kept within bounds by weeding out the suckers. It is charming when trained along a garden wall, and it is also lovely when grafted high and grown in the form of a standard. The stock on which the graft is made is black locust.

Rose-Acacia thrives in any well-drained soil and prefers a sunny location. It is easy to transplant, grows rapidly, and is readily increased by suckers. *R. Kelseyi,* Zone V, is indigenous to North Carolina; it is a taller form, growing to about nine feet. It is a beautiful species with masses of rose-pink flowers in May or June.

Rubus Odoratus, Zone III, Flowering Raspberry, is a shrub of minor importance. It is best suited to naturalistic plantings and abounds in moist, shady situations. It is also often seen growing along the roadside in both sun and shade. In cultivation it adapts itself to various soils, but it shows a preference for those that are rich and moist, and it particularly likes partly shady places. It grows to six feet or more. The purple flowers appear in July and are followed by red fruit. The supply can be increased by suckers.

Salix, Willow, surprising though it may seem, is available in a number of dwarf forms that are useful to small home owners. In their native haunts Willows grow luxuriantly in wet, swampy ground; the tree forms absorb and transpire quantities of water. The shrub-like types are chiefly planted in swampy, damp ground, where the choice of plant material is limited; however, they adapt themselves to various situations. Propagation is easily accomplished by cuttings. *S. caprea* can be increased by air-layers.

S. caprea, Zone IV, Goat Willow, grows to twenty-five feet in height. It produces showy catkins, Pussy Willows, that are larger than those of *S. discolor.*

S. discolor, Zone II, the well-known Pussy Willow, is a shrub or small tree ten to twenty feet tall. It grows satisfactorily in dry soil. Among the dwarf species are *S. helvetica,* Zone V (one to two feet high).

S. myrsinites, Zone IV (one and a half feet tall); and *S. purpurea var. nana,* Dwarf Purple Osier Willow. This is compact, hardy, with blue-gray foliage; it is a good plant for a low hedge in moist ground.

Sorbaria, False Spirea, is a member of the Rose Family; formerly it was included with the Spireas. This shrub is not fastidious as to soil, and it will grow in sun or light shade. The large, creamy-white flower plumes appear in July and August. It is not an appropriate bush for the small garden and is best used in masses on spacious lawns.

S. Aitchisoni, Zone (V), VI, grows to nine feet in height; it has red stems and ornamental foliage. Propagation is by suckers and cuttings.

S. sorbifolia, Zone II, is six feet high; it spreads rapidly by means of suckers.

Spirea Vanhouttei forms a graceful background for the perennial border. *Photographer, the Roches.*

Spiraea, Spirea, is numbered among the best-known and most ornamental groups of flowering shrubs for use in the home garden. They are grown principally for their showy, abundant, white, pink, or carmine flower clusters; these are produced from April into August, depending upon the species. They are low or medium-size shrubs, many of them graceful in habit. The foliage is rather small and gives a good effect all season.

The cultivation of Spireas is of the simplest. They will grow in almost any garden soil provided it is not too dry, but they prefer one that is moist and fertile. A sunny location is best, but they will tolerate light shade. The early-blooming kinds that flower from April through May, such as the Bridal Wreath, Thunberg, and Vanhoutte, should be pruned immediately after bloom. The summer flowering species—as for example Douglasii, Bumalda, and Margaritae—should be trimmed after bloom or in early spring before growth starts. Propagation is by cuttings of the growing wood taken in summer, by hardwood cuttings, layers, and seeds stratified as soon as ripe.

Aphids are apt to be troublesome, but they can be checked by one or more sprayings with Nicotine-sulphate or any other contact insecticide. There are many species of Spirea, some of which are given below.

S. albiflora, Zone IV, is a low-growing Japanese form that grows two feet high. The flowers are white and bloom in July and August.

S. arguta, Zone IV, is a showy, free-flowering kind that grows to about five feet. Its white blossoms appear in May.

S. Billiardii, Zone IV, is a gay plant with bright pink flowers in July and August. It is a compact shrub growing to six feet.

S. Bumalda Anthony Waterer is a low-growing shrub two feet tall, compact and shapely in its habit. The clusters of bright carmine flowers appear in July and August. Its blooming period is quite an extended one, provided the faded blooms are promptly removed. *S. Bumalda var. Normandie* is a dwarf form about five inches high. Its pink flowers come in May; in the fall the leaves turn bright red.

S. densiflora, Zone V, grows two feet high; it bears thick clusters of rose-colored blooms in June. This is a lovely, hardy shrub that tolerates temperatures to zero and slightly lower.

S. Douglasii, Zone IV, is a compact shrub to eight feet; its deep pink flowers are produced abundantly in July and August.

S. Margaritae attains a height of three to five feet. It is an ornamental species with good foliage and rather large bright pink flower clusters that open in late June or early July.

S. prunifolia var. plena, Bridal Wreath Spirea, is known to all gardeners. Its small, glossy foliage is attractive, and the profusion of small, white, double flowers crowd the branches in May. It attains a height of six feet; the leaves turn orange-scarlet in fall.

S Thunbergii, Zone IV, Thunberg Spirea, is from China and Japan; it grows to three or four feet, and although it is a hardy type, the tips of the branches are likely to winter-kill. This is the first Spirea to bloom; the small, white flowers appear in early April with the Daffodils and the Forsythias. It has finely divided foliage and is rather thin and open in habit. This species is one of the most popular.

S. Vanhouttei, Zone IV, is the most graceful and ornamental of all the species. Its arching branches are densely covered with white flower clusters in May. It grows about five feet tall.

Stephanandra Incisa, Zone IV, is a graceful, dense shrub seldom over five feet in height. It is grown chiefly for its attractive, finely divided foliage. This plant makes a lovely specimen and is also a useful subject for the mixed shrubbery border. The white flowers, although small, are borne profusely in June. When the young leaves first appear in the spring, they have a reddish hue; as they develop, the color changes to dark, glossy green. As fall approaches, the color changes again, turning to coppery shades of reddish-purple.

Stephanandra has no special requirements, thriving in practically any garden soil that is well-drained. Propagation is by layers or by cuttings taken in summer from the growing wood.

Stewartia is an outstanding summer-flowering shrub or tree. In common with Camellia and the Franklin Tree, it is a member of the Tea Family. Its large cup-shaped white flowers measure three to four inches across and resemble those of its relatives. They bloom in July and August. The foliage effect is excellent—the leaves are bright green in color, changing in the fall to vivid shades of orange and crimson.

A sheltered, sunny situation will prove ideal. *Stewartia* does best in soil that is moist and that contains an ample supply of leaf mold or peat moss. Propagation is by layers and by cuttings of the half-ripe wood taken in August and rooted under glass.

Before planting. *Courtesy Mahoney Construction Co. Photographer,*
Bill Harris.

The new planting as it appeared six months later. *Owners, Mr. and*
Mrs. Donald T. Ebert. Photographer, Bill Harris.

S. ovata, Zone V (*S. pentagyna*), is a vigorous upright shrub six to fifteen feet tall. Although a native of the mountain regions of Virginia and southward, it is hardy as far north as Massachusetts. *S. ovata* is the species most generally planted. *S. ovata grandiflora* differs from the other species because of its purple stamens, which contrast effectively with the large white flowers. It grows approximately ten to fifteen feet high.

S. Malacodendron, Zone VII, also a native species, grows to about eighteen feet. Its flowers sometimes measure four inches across.

Styrax Japonica, Zone V, Storax, Snowbell, is a tree-like shrub or small tree which ordinarily does not reach a height of more than fifteen feet; however, it sometimes grows to twenty-five feet. In late May or June the undersides of the branches are laden with clusters of white bell-shaped flowers that fall gracefully along the branches. *Styrax* makes a distinctive lawn specimen; it should be planted by itself where it has ample space for full development. Its dense habit of growth and its foliage effect are excellent.

A light, moist, but well-drained soil suits it best; in the North a protected location is advisable. *Styrax* can easily be raised from seed sown as soon as ripe—in fact, it frequently seeds itself. Cuttings root with difficulty; layering is the method generally employed when the plant fails to seed itself.

S. Obassia, Zone V, and *S. japonica,* Zone V, are the only species that are hardy enough to be grown in the North. The flowers of *S. Obassia* are very fragrant; it eventually grows to thirty feet. The other species, *S. Wilsonii,* Zone VII, grows to nine feet, and *S. grandifolia,* Zone VII, reaches twelve feet in height; its flowers are fragrant. Both of these grow in the milder climates.

Symphoricarpos Albus (*racemosus*), Zone III, Snowberry, has round, large, pure white fruit that is the distinctive feature of this shrub. In fact, there are few bushes that produce conspicuous white berries; these crowd the graceful branches in fall and persist on the plant until early winter.

The Snowberry is a slender low shrub two to three feet in height. Its bright green foliage has no special interest, and the small, pinkish flower clusters which appear in June are not particularly ornamental. It is not until the showy fruits come in late August or September that this shrub becomes effective.

Symphoricarpos will grow in sun or partial shade, and it will thrive in any soil—even poor, gravelly banks or heavy clay. It is a useful bush for clump plantings in semi-shady situations where many shrubs will not succeed; it can also be planted as a facer to taller bushes.

Unfortunately, *Symphoricarpos* is not entirely pest-free. Aphids and San Jose scale sometimes give trouble. A fungus disease, spot anthracnose, also attacks it and causes the berries to shrink, turn brown, and dry up. When this occurs, prune out all dead wood; the following spring spray with Ferbam, using two and a half tablespoons to one gallon of water; apply this as the buds unfold. Aphids are controlled with repeated sprayings of a nicotine preparation. San Jose scale is combatted with a dormant spray of Lime-sulphur or miscible oil. Propagation is by suckers, seeds, and division.

S. orbiculatus (*vulgaris*), Zone II, Indian Currant, Coralberry, grows two to three feet tall; it bears a profusion of dark-red fruit, which makes this shrub a very decorative one for fall and early winter effect.

Symplocos Paniculata, Zone V, Sapphire-berry, has beautiful blue berries, but they cannot be depended upon for fall effect since they are perishable and do not last long. The fragrant, small white flowers of this shrub appear in June; the blooming period is a short one, and the flowers are not showy. *Symplocos* usually does not exceed fifteen feet, although sometimes it grows much taller. It likes a sunny, well-drained situation and will thrive in any soil of average fertility. Propagation is by air-layers and by cuttings of the growing wood rooted under glass.

This Common Lilac (*Syringa vulgaris*) is an example of a well-grown specimen. The blooms cover the shrub almost to its base. *Photographer, the Roches.*

Chapter XV

Flowering Shrubs—Sy through Z

Syringa, Lilac, has captured the hearts of all garden lovers. Who can resist its beauty and fragrance? Indeed no home seems quite complete without its Lilac bush. Just as the rose belongs to June, the Lilac belongs to May—that enchanting month that brings with it a wealth of beauty.

The Common Lilac (*S. vulgaris*), native to the southern part of Europe, especially to Hungary and the mountain regions of Bulgaria, found its way into Turkey where it became a favorite garden plant. In the sixteenth century it was brought to Vienna from Turkey, and it made its appearance in England during the reign of Queen Elizabeth. In Raymond L. Taylor's *Plants of Colonial Days* we learn that in 1737 Peter Collinson sent Lilacs from England to John Bartram in Philadelphia.

In Colonial days Lilacs blossomed in the dooryard gardens, clothed the bare walls of the barns, and grew beside the spring houses. Hedges of Lilacs bordered the rural roadside. Everywhere Lilacs—symbol of spring—were treasured plants. The charm of their blooms, together with their ability to withstand severe cold and lack of care, is undoubtedly responsible for their universal popularity.

With the exception of the Deep South, Lilacs can be grown throughout this country and in parts of Canada. They are shrubs that like to be cold in winter and warm in summer, and they will grow in well-drained soils of average fertility. However, a properly fertilized, well-prepared soil and a sunny location will provide ideal growing conditions. If the earth is not rich, replace it with top-soil or compost; work well-rotted cow manure into the soil and sprinkle a little lime over the surface of the planting area. Lilacs can be moved either in fall or spring.

Each spring, fertilize the bushes with a complete commercial fertilizer, bone flour, or cottonseed meal. Every two years or so, dust the soil lightly with lime. A summer mulch of well-rotted cow manure is very beneficial. If this is not available, substitute leaf mold or peat moss. To counteract acidity, add a little lime.

Pruning Lilacs is an important part of the culture. They should be pruned immediately after bloom. Branches that crowd or cross each other should be pruned out, and the faded flowers should be removed with short stems. If Lilacs are cut for house decoration, this will give about the correct amount of pruning, provided the flowers are gathered with stems that are not too long. The growth of superfluous suckers saps the vitality of the shrub unnecessarily, and for this reason most of them should be removed. However, by retaining a few of them the supply of young growth will be maintained; as these develop, the older branches can be eliminated.

If pruning is neglected, the bushes become overgrown with old, unproductive wood; furthermore they grow too tall and out of bounds, and generally deteriorate. This condition should never be allowed to occur, but when it exists, renovation of the shrub becomes a necessity. This is done in early spring before growth starts. The shrub can be cut to within a foot from the ground, or the branches can be pruned back drastically. In either case, bloom cannot be expected for two or more years, since the new growth which develops will be too young to set flower buds. The exact time to expect flowers will depend upon the age of the wood that has been cut back. The wisest course to pursue is to bring about the rejuvenation gradually, over a two- to four-year period, depending upon the size and age of the shrub. Removing the old branches by degrees encourages the growth of enough suckers to replace their loss.

The usual question asked is: "Why don't my Lilacs bloom?" There is no reason for Lilacs not to bloom provided they are old enough to do so. These shrubs cannot be expected to flower until they are at least four feet high. If the plants are old enough and fail to set flower buds, it is because of faulty culture. One of the causes is improper pruning. Next year's flower buds commence to form immediately after the blooming period, and pruning should be attended to just as soon as the flowers fade. The branches should not be cut too severely unless renovation is in order. By practicing a little root pruning, bloom can sometimes be induced. This is done by opening a trench to the depth of a spading fork, and ten or twelve inches wide. The trench is made a little distance from the main stems of the bush. A generous layer of well-rotted cow manure is placed in the bottom of the trench before it is refilled with soil. If manure is not available, mix superphosphate in the soil as it is replaced. Deficiency in available plant food or planting in partial shade may also account for lack of bloom. Too rich a soil will sometimes cause a vegetative growth at the expense of the flowers; root pruning should help to remedy this condition. Excessive vegetative growth can be detected by an over-production of succulent shoots.

Lilacs are subject to some pests, among them being borers. If small mounds of sawdust are found on the ground during May or June, you may be sure that the enemy is at work. If the affected branches can be spared, cut them out and burn them. Otherwise it will be necessary to inject into the borer holes Carbon Bisulphide or some other preparation on the market for controlling borers. To prevent the pest, spray about the first of May with DDT or Malathion and repeat the spray once or twice at two-week intervals. Lilacs are also susceptible to scale; this can be eliminated by using a dormant spray of Lime-sulphur or miscible oil (see page 32).

Bacterial blight sometimes attacks the plants, causing black or brown spots on the leaves; it is very difficult to control. If the shrub is dense, prune out some of the center branches in order to improve the circulation of air. Cut out and burn all affected parts. After using the pruning shears, disinfect them in denatured alcohol to prevent spreading the disease. Two or three sprayings with Bordeaux applied in the spring can be tried.

Mildew disfigures the foliage. It is not a serious disease, but it is hard to conquer. It may help to spray with Mildex or Wettable Sulphur.

The easiest way to propagate Lilacs is by detaching rooted suckers from the plants. These are nursed along in an out-of-the-way spot until they are sufficiently large to be planted permanently.

Syringa vulgaris, Zone III, and its numerous varieties, is the most important species in cultivation. This Lilac blooms early and in great profusion; the blossoms of most of the varieties are extremely fragrant. Through the skill of Lemoine and other plant breeders, the garden-maker today has a bewildering array of varieties from which to choose. These come in shades of blue, lilac, purple, red, pink, and white, and in both single and double flowering forms. These hybrids are generally referred to as *French Lilacs,* or *French Hybrids,* and include such favorites as Edith Cavell (white, double); Ellen Wilmott (white, double); Mont Blanc (white, single); Vestale (white, single); Pres. Grevy (lilac,

Before planting. *Photographer, Paul E. Genereux.*

double); Victor Lemoine (lilac, double); Ludwig Spaeth (purple, single); Congo (burgundy, single); Charles Joly (reddish-purple, double).

The varieties given us by W. B. Clarke of San Jose, California, include the lovely blue Clarke's Giant, the pink Esther Staley, and Pink Spray. Holland has given us a pale-yellow Lilac, Primrose, which is a rather recent introduction in this country.

S. persica, Zone V, Persian Lilac, is of Asiatic origin and was introduced into England in the seventeenth century. It is a shrub of singular beauty, with a graceful, airy habit of growth. When it is properly cared

A flagstone walk with grass joints leads to the entrance that is marked each side with a handsome Yew. *Photographer, Paul E. Genereux.*

for, it produces a great profusion of fragrant blooms. The leaves are smaller than those of the Common Lilac, and it is lower growing (six feet) than other species. The Persian Lilac and the Common Lilac are excellent selections for the home owner who does not care to pay the price for the *French Lilacs*. They are both fragrant.

The varieties that were originated by Miss Isabella Preston of Ottawa, Canada, are noteworthy among the newer hybrids. They are a cross between *S. villosa* and *S. reflexa*. This group has been named *Prestoniae* after its originator. Among these varieties might be mentioned Isabella, Donald Wyman, and Miranda. The flowers of this group come in shades of pink; the blooming period is in June. The growth is compact and upright and attains a height of about eight feet.

There are various other species which are of particular interest to the gardener who wants to specialize in growing Lilacs. They are handsome, large shrubs with beautiful flowers, but some of these have little or no fragrance. A few of them are given below:

S. chinensis, Zone V, sometimes called the Rouen Lilac, is the oldest of the hybrids. It first appeared at the Botanic Gardens in Rouen in 1777. It is a cross between *S. vulgaris* and *S. persica*. Its flowers come in purple, white, and lilac-red. It grows ten to twelve feet high. This Chinese species requires little pruning—consisting chiefly of thinning the bushes and keeping them shapely.

S. microphylla, Zone V, is a Chinese species which grows into a broadly spreading shrub six feet high. It has small leaves and pale lilac flowers. Its distinguishing feature is that sometimes a few flowers are produced in the fall.

S. swegiflexa, Pink Pearl Lilac, has a compact habit of growth and reaches a height of about seven feet. The fragrant pink flowers are red in bud. It blooms in June, and for this reason it is of value in prolonging the flowering period.

S. villosa, Zone II, comes from northern China and is of particular interest to northern gardeners because of its hardiness. It comes into flower in early June when most Lilacs have finished blooming. It is a dense grower to ten feet. The lilac-pink flowers are not fragrant.

Tamarix, Tamarisk, is of chief value for use in seashore gardens where it grows luxuriantly. It has slender branches with feathery, diminutive pale-green leaves. The delicate pink flowers are borne in loose racemes and give a light, graceful effect. The habit of growth is open and lacks

This green garden has been designed and planted by the owners. The background of trees gives welcome shade in summer and the evergreens provide interest at all seasons. Box borders the unbroken lawn area. A small formal garden on the lower level requires practically no upkeep; *Pachysandra* which fills the beds have been grown from cuttings. The soft shades of the old bricks used for paving give effective color contrast with the evergreens. *Owners, Mr. and Mrs. William A. Randall. Courtesy Horticulture Magazine. Photographer, the Roches.*

symmetry; this characteristic can be partly overcome by pruning. If the branches are cut back each year, a shrubby, more stocky growth will be encouraged. Tamarisk thrives in sandy, gravelly soils and fails to grow well in heavy ground. The plants can be increased by seed and by cuttings taken from the growing wood.

T. odessana, Zone IV, is the lowest-growing species and the best for small gardens. It attains a height of six feet and is easy to keep adequately trimmed. Pruning should be done in early spring before growth starts, because the flowers are borne on wood of the current season's growth. This is an interesting shrub to include in the planting for a touch of the unusual. In July it is very attractive when the branches are covered with pretty pink flowers.

T. parviflora, Zone IV, blooms in late May. It should be pruned immediately after bloom, because the flowers form on wood of the previous season's growth. It reaches a height of fifteen feet.

Vaccinium, Blueberry, forms a genus of shrubs, both evergreen and deciduous, which can be found growing in the Arctic Circle and in the mountain regions of the tropics. The different species of Vaccinium have the various common names of Blueberry, Cranberry, Cowberry, and Whortleberry. It is sometimes incorrectly named Huckleberry, which belongs to the genus Gaylussacia.

Some of the Blueberries are raised especially for their delicious fruit; others, for their bright red autumn coloration of the foliage. All kinds require an acid soil, and some like it to be moist and sandy. Propagation is by division, layers, and cuttings.

V. corymbosum, Zone III, Highbush Blueberry, does not usually exceed six feet but can grow to twelve feet. This is one of the finest species for the home gardener. The clusters of dense, white flowers tinged with pink are borne in May or early June and are followed by blue-black berries. In the fall the foliage turns a vivid orange and scarlet, and the red twigs give winter color. When used in garden plantings, a mulch of peat moss will be beneficial. Varieties of this species have been developed to produce the delicious blueberries sold in markets.

V. angustifolium, Zone II (*V. pensylvanicum*), Lowbush Blueberry, is a small shrub which usually is not higher than one foot. This species does well on hillsides that are sandy and dry, and it can be used as a cover for land that is too poor for most plants. It is also adapted to underplant-

An entrance planting of Yews looks its best at all seasons. *Photographer, J. Horace McFarland Company.*

ing in wooded lots. It is not ornamental for the garden and is only suitable for mass plantings. The berries are bluish-black, and the foliage turns red in the fall.

Viburnum offers such splendid possibilities for home garden plantings that it is unusual not to find at least one of these noteworthy shrubs included in any planting scheme. The many species available to garden-makers differ widely in height, habit of growth, bloom, and fruit. Many of them are of value for fall display, both for their berries and for the autumnal tints of their foliage.

The majority of Viburnums do best in sunny, well-drained locations and in soil that is moist and fertile. Some kinds will thrive in the shade; others be grown in dry soil. The lover of fragrance will find this delightful quality in some of the species. The Viburnums are excellent subjects for the shrubbery borders, foundation plantings, and for use as

specimens. The taller-growing types are well adapted to boundary plantings and to screening purposes. In fact, wherever shrubs are planted a
Viburnum can be found that will fill the particular requirement.

The snowball aphis starts work early in spring; in most instances the
leaves are already curled before this pest is detected. It can easily be
controlled by repeated sprayings with Malathion, commencing in early
spring. If the bushes have not yet been sprayed before the leaves begin
to curl and the shrubs are small in size, they can be treated by dipping
the affected parts in a mixture of Nicotine and soap.

Propagation is by seeds stratified or sown when they ripen; also by
cuttings taken from the greenwood or hardwood, by layers, or by
grafting.

V. acerifolium, Zone III, Dockmackie, Maple-leaved Viburnum, reaches
a height of about six feet. The leaf resembles a small maple leaf, and the
yellow-white flowers appear in June. The fruit is nearly black and not
very decorative; however, in the autumn the foliage turns rosy-purple.
This species is of no value except for use in dense shade.

V. alnifolium, Zone III, Hobble-bush, inhabits woodland regions of the
northern states. It is suitable for use in partly shady, moist situations,
where it reaches a height of about ten feet. The blooming period is in
May. The white flower clusters are showy, and the fruits which follow
are bright red, later turning to purple-black.

V. Burkwoodi, Zone V, Burkwood Viburnum, bears deliciously scented
flowers that appear in May; they are white-tinted flesh pink. The foliage
is dark green and turns deep red in the fall. This shrub is readily increased
by cuttings. It prefers a moist soil in which to grow and attains a height
of about six feet.

V. carlcephalum has been produced by crossing *V. Carlesii* with *V.
macrocephalum.* It is a choice, fragrant shrub that reaches about seven
feet in height and is said to have withstood temperatures below zero.

V. Carlesii, Zone IV, Mayflower Viburnum, is a handsome Korean
species five or six feet high. Its blooming season is in May, and its fragrant flowers are pink in bud, changing to white when fully open. Since
all the blooms do not unfold at the same time, the contrast of the pink
buds with the white, fully blown flowers is effective. This shrub has a
round, compact habit and is a splendid plant for the small garden.

V. cassinoides, Zone III, Withe-rod, does not usually exceed six feet. The

In this bird sanctuary the figure of Saint Francis is framed with shrubbery. *Photographer, the Roches.*

creamy-white blooms are followed by clusters of berries that change in color from yellowish to red and finally to black. The leaves turn a brilliant red in the autumn. The plant grows in sun or in partial shade.

V. dentatum, Zone II, Arrow-wood, grows rapidly and attains a height of ten to fifteen feet. This species can easily be recognized by the markedly dentate margins of the leaves. The flat flower clusters are abundantly produced in late May or early June. It is an excellent shrub for mass plantings in sunny or partly shady locations. The blue-black berries are not particularly showy. The foliage changes to dark red in the fall.

V. dilatatum, Zone V, Linden Viburnum, is a desirable ornamental shrub ten feet or so in height, which comes to our gardens from China and Japan. It is bushy and shapely in its habit, with showy, flat flower clusters in May or early June. These are followed by clusters of scarlet fruits of exceptionally decorative value, which persist late on the branches. In the autumn the foliage turns a dull red. The variety *xanthocarpum* is a yellow-berried form.

V. fragrans, Zone V, Fragrant Viburnum, is native to northern China; it has the distinction of being the earliest species to bloom; the white flowers are pink in bud, and they are very fragrant but smaller than those of *V. Carlesii.* North of New York the flower buds are apt to winter-kill.

V. Lentago, Zone II, Sheep-berry, Nanny-berry, is a tree-like shrub which sometimes reaches a height of thirty feet. The creamy-white flowers that come in May are followed by blue-black berries.

V. macrocephalum, Zone VI, Chinese Snowball, is a tall shrub, growing to twelve feet. It is not very hardy, and when grown in the colder latitudes should be planted in a somewhat sheltered situation; it likes a very fertile soil. The large clusters of flowers give a handsome effect. This species tolerates the winter temperatures as far north as Philadelphia, but it is essentially a mild climate shrub. In the South it is semi-evergreen.

V. Opulus, Zone III, European Cranberry-bush, is an extremely ornamental shrub which grows to about twelve feet in height. The large, flat flower clusters appear in May. The clusters of scarlet fruit persist on the branches throughout the winter, unless the birds denude the bushes. Because of its fruit it is an effective shrub to combine with evergreens for winter color. This plant is especially susceptible to aphids, which cause the leaves to curl; therefore it is important to watch for this pest from earliest spring and to spray with Malathion.

The white flowers of a specimen *Viburnum tomentosum sterile* stand
out effectively against an evergreen background. *Photographer, the
Roches.*

The variety *V. Opulus nanum* is a dwarf, dense shrub that grows to two feet in height. It does not flower, but it is good for low hedges and useful for restricted planting spaces. *V. Opulus xanthocarpum* is a form with yellow fruit.

V. prunifolium, Zone III, Black-Haw, is a native species usually about fifteen feet high, but sometimes reaching a height of thirty feet. The flower clusters which appear in May or early June are followed by a profusion of pendulous clusters of showy berries, which are pink at first, later changing to red and finally to dark blue as they mature. In the autumn the leaves turn scarlet.

V. Sargenti, Zone V or IV, is an Asiatic species similar to *V. Opulus* but more effective in bloom; its berries are red. The variety *flavum* is one of the few yellow-fruited kinds. It attains a height of about ten feet.

V. setigerum, Zone (V) (*V. theiferum*), Tea Viburnum, is given the latter name because in China the Buddhist monks make an infusion from the leaves which is called Sweet Tea. The flowers of this species are followed by clusters of conspicuous red fruits, which give a splendid effect. The plant grows about twelve feet high, and is one of the best of the Chinese introductions. The variety *aurantiacum* has orange-yellow fruit.

V. tomentosum, Zone IV, has an attractive habit of growth with spreading branches that form almost horizontal tiers; this species makes an excellent specimen. It comes to us from China and Japan and is one of the most decorative and popular of the Viburnums. It grows into a broad bush about eight to ten feet high; the large flat flower clusters are borne along the branches in May. The fruit is red, changing to blue-black.

V. tomentosum sterile (*V. tomentosum var. plicatum*), Japanese Snowball, is widely planted because of its large, showy blooms, good foliage, and attractive form. The flowers are sterile—no berries are produced. The shrub is of Japanese origin and is the best for use in cold climates.

Vitex Agnus-Castus, Zone (VI) or VII, Hemp-tree, Monks Peppertree, Chaste-tree, is one of the loveliest of the late summer flowering shrubs. Its long spikes of lavender-blue, fragrant flowers crowd the branches in August and September. The divided leaves are rich green with gray-green on the undersides; they are of special interest because of their aromatic fragrance when crushed. Since they do not leaf out until the weather becomes warm and settled, it is sometimes mistakenly thought to have winter-killed.

Vitex is not overly hardy; and where winters are cold, the branches are apt to die back severely. In common with *Buddleia,* new shoots appear in spring and flower the same year. Where climatic conditions are favorable this shrub attains a height of approximately nine feet. Inasmuch as it is a heavy grower, it is best to plant it by itself as a background shrub or along a fence line. A sunny location in practically any soil will supply its needs, provided the ground is well-drained. Propagation is by layers and by cuttings taken from the growing wood. The variety *rosea* is a pink-flowered type; the variety *alba* bears white blooms.

Shrubs as an underplanting to trees give privacy from the neighboring house. *Photographer, Paul E. Genereux.*

V. Agnus-castus latifolia (*V. macrophylla*) is hardier and more vigorous than *V. Agnus-castus*. It produces decorative spikes of blue flowers. If cut back to within a foot from the ground each spring before growth starts, the bush can be kept lower and more compact; when given this treatment, it will qualify for use in the mixed border.

V. Negundo is a Chinese species about fifteen feet tall; its panicles of lavender flowers are rather open in effect. The variety *V. Negundo incisa,* Zone (V), is an attractive cut-leaved form that is hardier and more graceful in habit.

Weigela, Diervilla, is one of the most popular and ornamental of the flowering shrubs. The profusion of flowers that are borne along its branches appear in late May or early June and transform the shrub into a bower of bloom. *Weigela* is not reliably hardy north of New York. In severe climates the branches are apt to die-back; therefore northern gardeners should select a protected situation for this plant.

Weigela reaches a height of five to ten feet. However, since it can be kept within bounds by pruning, it is an excellent shrub for the small place. Pruning should be done immediately after the blooming period; this consists of trimming back the long ends of the branches and keeping the old wood cut out. *Weigela* is easy to grow and will thrive in any garden soil that is not excessively dry. It prefers the full sun. If grown in the partial shade, it will not bloom so generously and will tend to become straggly.

The best *Weigelas* to select are the named varieties of hybrids which are listed by nurserymen. The flowers come in white, pink, and red. Among these are Fairy (pink), Bristol Ruby (red), Eva Rathke (red), and Candida (white). Certain types are available with variegated leaves.

Zenobia Pulverulenta, Zone V, is a handsome, compact deciduous or partly evergreen shrub which grows four to six feet in height. Its native habitat is from North Carolina to Florida. Its clusters of nodding, bell-shaped, white flowers bloom in May and June. The gray-green foliage gives this bush an unusual appearance and provides sharp contrast when planted with all-green shrubs. The leaves turn red in the fall and add cheer to the autumnal days.

In common with other members of the Heath Family (Ericaceae), *Zenobia* thrives best in sandy, peaty soil which is free from lime. Propagation is by seeds and by layers.

Part IV

LISTS OF SHRUBS FOR
VARIOUS LOCATIONS AND USES

FRAGRANT SHRUBS

Abelia grandiflora (Arbutus-bush, Glossy Abelia)
Abeliophyllum distichum (Korean Abelia-leaf)
Azalea arborescens (Sweet Azalea)
Azalea canescens
Azalea atlanticum
Azalea rosea (Roseshell Azalea)
Azalea Schlippenbachii (Royal Azalea)
Azalea viscosa (Swamp Azalea)
Azalea yodogava
Buddleia alternifolia (Butterfly-bush)
Buddleia Davidi (Butterfly-bush)
Buxus suffruticosa (Dwarf Box)
Calycanthus floridus (Carolina Allspice)
Cephalanthus occidentalis (Button bush)
Chionanthus virginicus (Fringe-tree)
Clethra alnifolia (Summersweet)
Corylopsis glabrescens (Winter-hazel)
Cytisus nigricans (Broom)
Daphne Burkwoodi (Somerset)
Daphne Cneorum (Rose Daphne, Garland Flower)
Daphne Mezereum (February Daphne)
Dipelta floribunda
Elaeagnus angustifolia (Russian Olive)
Elaeagnus commutata (Silver-berry Elaeagnus)
Elaeagnus multiflora
Elaeagnus pungens (Oleaster)
Erica arborea
Franklinia alatamaha (Franklin Tree)
Hamamelis mollis (Chinese Witch-hazel)
Hamamelis vernalis (Witch-hazel)
Itea virginica (Virginia Willow)
Jasminum nudiflorum (Jasmine)
Ledum
Lindera Benzoin (Spice-bush)
Lonicera fragrantissima (Winter Honey-suckle)
Lonicera Maacki (Amur Honeysuckle)
Lonicera microphylla (Honeysuckle)
Lonicera nitida (Box Honeysuckle)
Lonicera pileata (Privet Honeysuckle)
Lonicera spinosa (Honeysuckle)
Lonicera syringantha (Lilac Honeysuckle)

Lonicera syringantha var. wolfi (Honey-suckle)
Lonicera thibetica (Honeysuckle)
Magnolia stellata (Star Magnolia)
Myrica pensylvanica (Bayberry)
Osmanthus ilicifolius (Holly Osmanthus)
Philadelphus Avalanche (Mock Orange)
Philadelphus Belle Etoile (Mock Orange)
Philadelphus Boule d'Argent (Mock Orange)
Philadelphus Candelabra (Mock Orange)
Philadelphus coronarius (Sweet Mock Orange, Common Mock Orange)
Philadelphus Innocence (Mock Orange)
Philadelphus Mont Blanc (Mock Orange)
Philadelphus Perle Blanche (Mock Orange)
Philadelphus virginal (Mock Orange)
Poncirus trifoliata (Hardy Orange)
Rosa centifolia (Cabbage Rose)
Rosa centifolia muscosa (Moss Rose)
Rosa Cinnamomea (Cinnamon Rose)
Rosa damascena (Damask Rose)
Rosa Eglanteria (rubiginosa) leaves (Sweet Brier Rose)
Rosa Gallica (French Rose)
Rosa Harisoni (Harison's Yellow Rose)
Rosa Max Graf
Rosa Wichuriana (Memorial Rose)
Sarcococca confusa (Sweet Box)
Sarococca Hookeriana humilis
Sarcococca ruscifolia (Fragrant Sarcococca)
Skimmia japonica
Styrax grandiflora (Storax, Snowbell)
Styrax Obassia
Symplocos paniculata (Sapphire-berry)
Syringa in variety (Lilac)
Viburnum Burkwoodi (Burkwood Viburnum)
Viburnum carlcephalum
Viburnum Carlesii (Mayflower Viburnum)
Viburnum fragrans (Fragrant Viburnum)
Vitex Agnus-castus var. latifolia (V. macrophylla) — (Chaste-tree)

SHRUBS THAT WILL GROW
IN PARTIAL SHADE

Acanthopanax pentaphyllus
Amelanchier canadensis (Shadbush, Shadblow, Service-berry)
Amorpha fruticosa (False Indigo)
Aralia spinosa (Hercules' Club)
Arctostaphylos uva-ursi (Bearberry)
Aucuba japonica (Japanese Aucuba)
Azalea in variety
Buxus sempervirens (Common Box)
Callicarpa Bodinieri Giraldii (Beautyberry)
Callicarpa japonica (Beauty-berry)
Callicarpa dichotoma (C. purpurea) (Beauty-berry)
Calycanthus floridus (Carolina Allspice)
Cephalanthus occidentalis (Button bush)
Cercis canadensis (Redbud Judas-tree)
Chionanthus virginicus (Fringe-tree)
Clethra alnifolia (Summersweet)
Cornus in variety (Dogwood)
Cotoneaster Dammeri
Daphne Mezereum (February Daphne)
Enkianthus campanulatus (Redvein Enkianthus)
Enkianthus perulatus
Euonymus Fortunei Carrieri
Euonymus Fortunei kewensis
Euonymus Fortunei minima
Euonymus Fortunei radicans
Euonymus patens
Forsythia in variety (Golden-bell)
Fothergilla Gardeni
Fothergilla major
Fothergilla monticola
Gaylussacia (Huckleberry)
Hamamelis vernalis (Witch-hazel)
Hamamelis virginiana (Witch-hazel)
Hedera Helix (English Ivy)
Hydrangea arborescens grandiflora (Hills-of-Snow)
Hydrangea paniculata grandiflora (Peegee Hydrangea)
Hydrangea quercifolia (Oak-leaved Hydrangea)
Hydrangea Sargentiana (Sargent Hydrangea)
Hypericum in variety (St. John's-wort)
Ilex crenata (Japanese Holly)
Ilex glabra (Inkberry)
Itea virginica (Virginia Willow)

Kalmia latifolia (Mountain Laurel)
Kerria japonica (Kerria)
Laburnum (Golden Chain)
Ledum
Leucothoe Catesbaei (Drooping Leucothoe)
Ligustrum in variety (Privet)
Lindera Benzoin (Spice-bush)
Lonicera fragrantissima (Winter Honeysuckle)
Lonicera Ledebourii (Ledebour Honeysuckle)
Mahonia in variety (Oregon Holly-grape)
Nandina domestica (Heavenly Bamboo)
Osmanthus ilicifolius (Holly Osmanthus)
Pachistima Canbyi (Canby Pachistima)
Pachysandra (Japanese Spurge)
Philadelphus in variety (Mock Orange)
Physocarpos opulifolius (Ninebark)
Pieris floribunda (Mountain Andromeda)
Pieris japonica (Japanese Pieris)
Prunus Laurocerasus (Cherry Laurel)
Pyracantha coccinea (Firethorn)
Rhododendron carolinianum (Carolina Rhododendron)
Rhododendron maximum (Rosebay Rhododendron)
Rhodotypos scandens (R. kerrioides) (White Kerria, Jet-Bead)
Rubus odoratus (Flowering Raspberry)
Sarcococca confusa (Sweet Box)
Sarcococca Hookeriana humilis
Sarcococca ruscifolia (Fragrant Sarcococca)
Skimmia japonica
Sorbaria (False Spirea)
Symphoricarpos orbiculatus (Indian Currant, Coralberry)
Taxus canadensis var. stricta (Yew)
Vaccinium angustifolium (Lowbush Blueberry)
Vaccinium ovatum (Evergreen Blueberry)
Viburnum acerifolium (Dockmackie, Maple-leaved)
Viburnum cassinoides (Withe-rod)
Viburnum dentatum (Arrow-wood)
Viburnum tinus (Laurestinus) var. lucidum
Vinca minor (Myrtle, Periwinkle)

SHRUBS FOR DRY SOILS

Acanthopanax pentaphyllus
Amorpha fruticosa (False Indigo)
Arctostaphylos uva-ursi (Bearberry)
Berberis Thunbergii (Japanese Barberry)
Calluna vulgaris (Heather)
Caragana arborescens (Pea-tree)
Cytisus scoparius (Scotch Broom)
Daphne Cneorum (Rose Daphne, Garland Flower)

Elaeagnus angustifolia (Russian Olive)
Erica in variety (Heath)
Gaylussacia baccata (Black Huckleberry)
Juniperus (Juniper)
Myrica pensylvanica (Bayberry)
Salix discolor (Pussy Willow)
Tamarix (Tamarisk)
Vaccinium angustifolium (Lowbush Blueberry)

SHRUBS FOR SWAMPY LAND

Amelanchier canadensis (Shadbush, Shadblow, Service-berry)
Aronia arbutifolia (Red Chokeberry)
Azalea viscosa (Swamp Azalea)
Cephalanthus occidentalis (Button Bush)
Chamaedaphne calyculata (Leather-leaf)
Clethra alnifolia (Summersweet)

Gaylussacia dumosa (Dwarf Huckleberry)
Hamamelis virginiana (Witch-hazel)
Ledum
Lindera Benzoin (Spice-bush)
Rosa palustris
Salix caprea (Goat Willow)
Salix discolor (Pussy Willow)

SHRUBS FOR SEASHORE PLANTING

Arctostaphylos uva-ursi (Bearberry)
Berberis Thunbergii (Japanese Barberry)
Chamaedaphne calyculata (Leather-leaf)
Clethra alnifolia (Summersweet)
Cytisus scoparius (Scotch Broom)
Elaeagnus angustifolia (Russian Olive)
Euonymus japonica
Euonymus patens
Gaylussacia (Huckleberry)
Genista
Hibiscus syriacus (Althaea, Rose of Sharon)
Hippophae rhamnoides (Sea-Buckthorn)
Hydrangea macrophylla Hortensia (Greenhouse Hydrangea)
Ilex glabra (Inkberry)

Ilex opaca (American Holly)
Itea virginica (Virginia Willow)
Juniperus Pfitzeriana
Ligustrum in variety (Privet)
Lonicera nitida (Box Honeysuckle)
Myrica pensylvanica (M. caroliniensis) — (Bayberry)
Prunus maritima (Beach Plum)
Rosa lucida (R. virginiana), (Virginia Rose)
Rosa nitida (Shining Rose)
Rosa rugosa
Rosa Wichuriana (Memorial Rose)
Spiraea in variety (Spirea)
Tamarix in variety (Tamarisk)
Vaccinium ovatum (Evergreen Blueberry)

SHRUBS FOR CITY YARDS

Acanthopanax pentaphyllus
Amorpha fruticosa (False Indigo)
Aralia spinosa (Hercules' Club)
Arctostaphylos uva-ursi (Bearberry)
Aucuba japonica (Japanese Aucuba)
Azalea in variety
Berberis in variety (Barberry)
Chaenomeles lagenaria (Flowering Quince)
Chamaedaphne calyculata (Leather-leaf)
Cornus alba sibirica (Siberian Dogwood)
Cornus stolonifera (Red-Osier Dogwood)
Deutzia in variety
Elaeagnus angustifolia (Russian Olive)
Euonymus in variety
Exochorda racemosa (Pearlbush)
Forsythia in variety (Golden-bell)
Hedera Helix (English Ivy)
Hibiscus syriacus (Althaea, Rose of
    Sharon)
Hydrangea macrophylla Hortensia
    (Greenhouse Hydrangea)
Ilex crenata in variety (Japanese Holly)
Kalmia (Laurel)
Laburnum (Golden Chain)
Ligustrum in variety (Privet)

Lonicera fragrantissima (Winter Honey-
    suckle)
Magnolia stellata (Star Magnolia)
Myrica pensylvanica (M. caroliniensis) —
    (Bayberry)
Nandina domestica (Heavenly Bamboo)
Osmanthus (Holly Osmanthus)
Philadelphus coronarius (Common Mock-
    Orange, Sweet Mock-Orange)
Pieris japonica (Japanese Pieris)
Pyracantha coccinea var. Lalandi (Fire-
    thorn)
Rhododendron hybrids
Rhodotypos scandens (R. kerrioides)
    (White Kerria, Jet-Bead)
Rosa in variety (Rose)
Skimmia japonica
Spiraea Vanhouttei (Vanhoutte Spirea)
Symphoricarpos in variety (Snowberry,
    Coralberry)
Syringa vulgaris (Common Lilac)
Taxus cuspidata (Yew)
Viburnum in variety
Weigela

SHRUBS SUITABLE FOR INFORMAL OR NATURALISTIC PLANTINGS

Acanthopanax pentaphyllus
Amelanchier canadensis (Shadbush, Shad-
    blow, Service-berry)
Aronia arbutifolia (Red Chokeberry)
Azalea in variety
Calluna vulgaris (Heather)
Cercis canadensis (Redbud Judas-tree)
Clethra alnifolia (Summersweet)
Cornus florida (Flowering Dogwood)
Cornus mas (Cornelian Cherry)
Cornus racemosa (Gray Dogwood)
Cytisus scoparius (Scotch Broom)
Erica in variety
Gaylussacia in variety (Huckleberry)
Hamamelis mollis (Chinese Witch-hazel)
Hamamelis vernalis (Witch-hazel)
Hamamelis virginiana (Witch-hazel)
Itea virginica (Virginia Willow)
Kalmia angustifolia (Sheep Laurel, Lamb-
    kill)

Kalmia latifolia (Mountain-Laurel)
Ledum
Leucothoe Catesbaei (Drooping Leu-
    cothoe)
Lindera Benzoin (Spice-bush)
Mahonia Aquifolium (Oregon Holly-
    grape)
Myrica caroliniensis (M. pensylvanica)
    (Bayberry)
Prunus maritima (Beach Plum)
Rhododendron maximum (Rosebay Rho-
    dodendron)
Rubus odoratus (Flowering Raspberry)
Symphoricarpos albus (Snowberry)
Symphoricarpos orbiculatus (Coral-berry,
    Indian Currant)
Vaccinium in variety (Blueberry)

SHRUBS SUITABLE FOR USE
AS GROUND COVERS

Arctostaphylos uva-ursi (Bearberry)
Calluna vulgaris (Heather)
Cotoneaster Dammeri
Cotoneaster horizontalis
Euonymus Fortunei colorata
Euonymus Fortunei kewensis
Euonymus Fortunei vegeta
Euonymus radicans acuta
Hedera Helix (English Ivy)
Hypericum calycinum (Aaron's-Beard, St. John's-wort)

Mahonia nervosa (shrubby) — (Cascades Mahonia)
Mahonia repens
Pachistima Canbyi (Canby Pachistima)
Pachysandra terminalis (Japanese Spurge)
Sarcococca Hookeriana humilis
Vaccinium angustifolium (pensylvanicum — (Lowbush Blueberry)
Vinca minor (Myrtle, Periwinkle)

DWARF AND LOW-GROWING SHRUBS

Amorpha canescens (Lead-plant)
Arctostaphylos uva-ursi (Bearberry)
Aronia melanocarpa (Black Chokeberry)
Azalea Kaempferi (Torch Azalea)
Azalea Kurume
Azalea mollis
Berberis pygmaea
Berberis pygmaea nana
Berberis verruculosa (Warty Barberry)
Buxus microphylla koreana (Korean Box)
Buxus myrtifolia (Myrtle-leaved Box)
Buxus sempervirens suffruticosa (Dwarf Box)
Calluna vulgaris (Heather)
Caragana (Pea-tree)
Chaenomeles japonica alpina
Chamaedapne calyculata (Leather-leaf)
Cotoneaster adpressa
Cotoneaster Dammeri
Cotoneaster horizontalis
Daphne Cneorum (Rose Daphne, Garland Flower)
Daphne Mezereum (February Daphne)
Erica carnea (Spring Heath)
Erica ciliaris (Fringed Heath)
Erica darleyensis
Euonymus Fortunei Carrieri
Euonymus Fortunei colorata
Euonymus Fortunei kewensis
Euonymus Fortunei minima
Forsythia intermedia var. nana (Golden-bell)
Forsythia viridissima Bronxensis (Golden-bell)
Gaylussacia baccata (Black Huckleberry)
Gaylussacia dumosa (Dwarf Huckleberry)
Genista germanica
Genista hispanica var. compacta
Genista radiata
Genista sagittalis
Genista tinctoria var. prostrata
Hypericum in variety (St. John's-wort)
Ilex crenata Green Cushion (Holly)

Ilex crenata Green Island (Holly)
Ilex crenata Helleri (Holly)
Ilex crenata Kingsville (Holly)
Ilex crenata microphylla (Littleleaf Japanese Holly)
Ilex crenata nummularia (Holly)
Ilex crenata Stokesi (Holly)
Juniperus chinensis Sargenti (Juniper)
Juniperus Douglasii (Juniper)
Juniperus horizontalis var. Bar Harbor (Juniper)
Juniperus procumbens (Juniper)
Kalmia angustifolia (Sheep-Laurel, Lamb-kill)
Ledum
Leucothoe Catesbaei (Drooping Leucothoe)
Ligustrum vulgare Lodense (Privet)
Lonicera pileata (Privet Honeysuckle)
Mahonia nervosa (Cascades Mahonia)
Pachistima Canbyi (Canby Pachistima)
Pachistima Myrsinites
Pachysandra terminalis (Japanese Spurge)
Pieris japonica var. pygmaea
Rosa nitida (Shining Rose)
Salix helvetica (Willow)
Salix myrsinites (Willow)
Salix purpurea var. nana (Dwarf Purple Osier Willow)
Sarcococca Hookeriana humilis
Spiraea albiflora (Spirea)
Spiraea Bumalda Anthony Waterer (Anthony Waterer Spirea)
Spiraea Bumalda var. Normandie (Spirea)
Symphoricarpos albus (Snowberry)
Taxus baccata var. repandens (Yew)
Taxus canadensis var. stricta (Yew)
Taxus cuspidata densa (Yew)
Taxus cuspidata nana (formerly T. brevifolia) — (Yew)
Vaccinium angustifolium (V. pensylvanicum) — (Lowbush Blueberry)
Viburnum Opulus var. nanum

SHRUBS OF VALUE FOR AUTUMN
COLORATION OF FOLIAGE

Acanthopanax pentaphyllus, yellow

Amelanchier, red or yellow (Shadbush, Shadblow, Service-berry)

Arctostaphylos uva-ursi, bronze (Bear-berry)

Aronia arbutifolia, red (Red Chokeberry)

Azalea Exbury hybrids, red or yellow

Azalea Kaempferi, orange and scarlet (Torch Azalea)

Azalea Schlippenbachii, red (Royal Azalea)

Azalea Vaseyi, red (Pinkshell Azalea)

Azalea viscosa, orange to bronze (Swamp Azalea)

Berberis in variety, red (Barberry)

Cercis canadensis, yellow (Redbud, Judas-tree)

Chaenomeles sinensis, red (Chinese Quince)

Clethra alnifolia, yellow (Summersweet)

Cornus alba sibirica, red (Siberian Dog-wood)

Cornus Amomum, red (Silky Dogwood)

Cornus florida, red (Flowering Dogwood)

Cornus Kousa, red (Japanese Flowering Dogwood)

Cornus mas, red (Cornelian Cherry)

Cotinus Coggygria, yellow (Smoke-tree)

Cotoneaster adpressa, red

Cotoneaster divaricata, red

Cotoneaster horizontalis, red

Enkianthus campanulatus, scarlet (Red-vein Enkianthus)

Enkianthus perulatus, partly red

Euonymus alata, deep rose (Winged Spin-dle-tree)

Euonymus americana, red (Strawberry-bush)

Euonymus europaea, red (European Spindle-tree)

Euonymus Fortunei colorata, red

Euonymus Fortunei radicans, reddish-purple

Euonymus latifolia, red

Euonymus sanguinea, red

Fothergilla Gardeni, yellow to red

Fothergilla major, yellow to scarlet

Franklinia alatamaha, scarlet to yellow (Franklin Tree)

Halesia carolina, yellow (Silverbell Tree)

Hamamelis, yellow (Witch-hazel)

Itea virginica, red (Virginia Willow)

Kerria japonica, yellow (Kerria)

Leucothoe Catesbaei, red and bronze (Drooping Leucothoe)

Lindera Benzoin, yellow (Spice-bush)

Magnolia stellata, bronze-yellow (Star Magnolia)

Mahonia aquifolium, red and bronze (Oregon Holly-grape)

Nandina domestica, red (Heavenly Bam-boo)

Pachistima Canbyi, red to purple (Canby Pachistima)

Poncirus trifoliata, yellow (Hardy-Orange)

Prinsepia sinensis, yellow

Rhus cotinus see Cotinus Coggygria

Rosa rugosa, red and yellow

Rosa setigera, red (Prairie Rose)

Spiraea Bumalda var. Normandie, red (Spirea)

Spiraea prunifolia, red to orange (Bridal-wreath Spirea)

Spiraea Thunbergii, yellow to orange (Thunberg Spirea)

Stephanadra incisa, red

Stewartia ovata grandiflora, orange to scar-let

Vaccinium angustifolium, red (Lowbush Blueberry)

Vaccinium corymbosum, scarlet (High-bush Blueberry)

Viburnum acerifolium, rosy-purple (Dock-mackie, Maple-leaved Viburnum)

Viburnum alnifolium, red (Hobble-bush, American Wayfaring-tree)

Viburnum Burkwoodi, red (Burkwood Vi-burnum)

Viburnum Carlesii, red to purple (May-flower Viburnum)

Viburnum cassinoides, red (Withe-rod)

Viburnum dentatum, dark red (Arrow-wood)

Viburnum dilatatum, dull red (Linden Vi-burnum)

Viburnum Opulus, red (European Cran-berry-bush)

Viburnum prunifolium, red (Black Haw)

Zenobia, red

SHRUBS TO ATTRACT BIRDS

Aralia spinosa (Hercules' Club)
Arctostaphylos uva-ursi (Bearberry)
Azalea nudiflora (Pinxterbloom Azalea)
Azalea viscosa (Swamp Azalea)
Callicarpa (Beauty-berry)
Cercis canadensis (Redbud, Judas-tree)
Chionanthus virginicus (Fringe-tree)
Clethra alnifolia (Summersweet)
Cornus in variety (Dogwood)
Elaeagnus angustifolia (Russian Olive)
Elaeagnus multiflora
Euonymus alata (Winged Spindle-tree)
Euonymus americana (Strawberry-bush)
Euonymus europaea (European Spindle-tree)
Gaylussacia baccata (Black Huckleberry)
Ilex (Holly)
Jasminum (Jasmine)
Juniperus horizontalis (Juniper)
Ligustrum vulgare (Common Privet)

Linders Benzoin (Spice-bush)
Lonicera in variety (Honeysuckle)
Mahonia Aquifolium (Oregon Holly-grape)
Mahonia nervosa (Cascades Mahonia)
Myrica (Bayberry)
Poncirus trifoliata (Hardy-orange)
Pyracantha coccinea (Firethorn)
Rosa carolina (Carolina Rose)
Rosa nitida (Shining Rose)
Rosa palustris
Rosa setigera (Prairie Rose)
Rosa virginiana (Virginia Rose)
Rubus (Flowering Raspberry)
Salix discolor (Pussy Willow)
Symphoricarpos albus (Snowberry)
Thuja occidentalis (American Arbor-vitae)
Tsuga canadensis (Hemlock)
Vaccinium in variety (Blueberry)
Viburnum in variety
Weigela hybrids in variety

SHRUBS WITH PINK OR ROSE-COLORED FRUITS

Cornus Kousa, pinkish (Japanese Flowering Dogwood)
Euonymus americana, salmon pink (Strawberry-bush)
Euonymus Bungeana var. semi-persitens, pink or yellow
Euonymus europaea, pink-orange (European Spindle-tree)
Euonymus latifolia, pink
Euonymus nana, pink (Dwarf Euonymus)
Euonymus patens, pink
Viburnum cassinoides, pink finally blue (Withe-rod)

SHRUBS WITH GRAY, SILVER OR WHITE FRUITS

Cornus alba sibirica, bluish white (Siberian Dogwood)
Cornus Amomum, blue or whitish (Silky Dogwood)
Cornus racemosa, white (Gray Dogwood)
Cornus stolonifera, white (Red-Osier Dogwood)
Daphne Genkwa, white
Elaeagnus commutata, silvery (Silverberry Elaeagnus)
Myrica pensylvanica (M. caroliniensis) gray (Bayberry)
Symphoricarpos albus, white (Snowberry)

SHRUBS WITH RED FRUITS

Arctostaphylos uva-ursi (Bearberry)
Aronia arbutifolia (Red Chokeberry)
Aucuba japonica (Japanese Aucuba)
Azalea Vaseyi (Pinkshell Azalea)
Berberis concinna (Barberry)
Berberis diaphana (Barberry)
Berberis koreana (Barberry)
Berberis mentorensis (Mentor Barberry)
Beberis Thunbergii (Japanese Barberry)
Berberis Vernae (Barberry)
Berberis vulgaris (Common Barberry)
Berberis Wilsonae (Barberry)
Cornus florida (Flowering Dogwood)
Cornus Kousa (Japanese Flowering Dogwood, red-pinkish)
Cornus mas (Cornelian Cherry)
Cotoneaster adpressa
Cotoneaster bullata var. floribunda
Cotoneaster Dammeri
Cotoneaster Dielsiana
Cotoneaster Francheti (orange red)
Cotoneaster horizontalis
Cotoneaster hupehensis
Cotoneaster multiflora
Cotoneaster racemiflora
Cotoneaster salicifolia var. floccosa
Daphne Mezereum (February Daphne)
Elaeagnus multiflora
Elaeagnus pungens (Oleaster)
Euonymus americana (Strawberry-bush)
Euonymus europaea (European Spindle-tree)
Euonymus Fortunei vegeta
Euonymus latifolia
Euonymus obovata (Running Strawberry-bush)
Euonymus sanguinea
Ilex aquifolium (English Holly)
Ilex cornuta (Chinese Holly)
Ilex cornuta Burfordi (Burford Holly)
Ilex opaca (American Holly)
Ilex pedunculosa (Long-stalk Holly)

Ilex Pernyi (Holly)
Ilex yunnanensis (Yunnan Holly)
Lindera Benzoin (Spice-bush)
Lonicera alpigena (Honeysuckle)
Lonicera alpigena var. nana (Honeysuckle)
Lonicera chrysantha (Honeysuckle)
Lonicera gracilipes (Spangle Honeysuckle)
Lonicera korolkowi (Blue-leaf Honeysuckle)
Lonicera prostrata (Honeysuckle)
Lonicera syringantha (Lilac Honeysuckle)
Lonicera tatarica (Tatarian Honeysuckle)
Lonicera tatarica parviflora (Orange-red Honeysuckle)
Lonicera thibetica (Honeysuckle)
Magnolia stellata (Star Magnolia)
Nandina domestica (Heavenly Bamboo)
Prinsepia uniflora
Pyracantha angustifolia (Firethorn)
Pyracantha coccinea (Firethorn)
Pyracantha coccinea var. Lalandi (orange to red) — (Firethorn)
Pyracantha crenulata (Firethorn)
Pyracantha Gibbsii (Firethorn)
Rosa carolina (Carolina Rose)
Rosa centifolia muscosa (Moss Rose)
Rosa rugosa (Rose)
Rosa virginiana (Virginia Rose)
Rubus odoratus (Flowering Raspberry)
Sarcococca ruscifolia (Fragrant Sarcococca)
Skimmia japonica
Symphoricarpos orbiculatus (Indian Currant, Coralberry)
Viburnum alnifolium (Hobble-bush)
Viburnum dilatatum (Linden Viburnum)
Viburnum Opulus (European Cranberry-bush)
Viburnum rhytidophyllum (red finally black) — (Leather-leaf Viburnum)
Viburnum Sargenti
Viburnum setigerum (Tea Viburnum)

SHRUBS WITH FRUIT IN SHADES
OF BLACK, BLUE AND PURPLE

Acanthopanax pentaphyllus, black
Aralia spinosa, black (Hercules' Club)
Berberis buxifolia, purple (Magellan Barberry)
Berberis Sargentiana, bluish black (Sargeant Barberry)
Berberis triacanthophora, blue black (Three-spine Barberry)
Berberis verruculosa, blue black (Warty Barberry)
Callicarpa Bodinieri Giraldii, violet (Beauty-berry)
Callicarpa dichotoma (C. purpurea) lilac-pink or mauve (Beauty-berry)
Chionanthus retusus, purplish blue
Chionanthus virginicus, blue (Fringe-tree)
Cornus Amomum, blue to whitish (Silky Dogwood)
Cotoneaster lucida, black
Cotoneaster melanocarpa, black
Cotoneaster nitens, purplish black
Gaylussacia baccata, black (Black Huckleberry)
Gaylussacia dumosa, black (Dwarf Huckleberry)
Ilex crenata, black (Japanese Holly)
Ilex crenata convexa, black (Convex-leaved Japanese Holly)
Ilex glabra, black (Inkberry)
Juniperus horizontalis, blue (Juniper)
Ligustrum acuminatum, black (Privet)
Ligustrum amurense, black (Amur Privet)
Ligustrum obtusifolium var. Regelianum, black (Regel Privet)
Ligustrum vulgare, black (Common Privet)
Lonicera Ledebourii, black (Ledebour Honeysuckle)
Lonicera nitida, blue purple (Box Honeysuckle)
Lonicera pileata, violet (Privet Honeysuckle)
Mahonia Aquifolium, blue black (Oregon Holly-grape)
Mahonia nervosa, purple (Cascades Mahonia)
Osmanthus Aquifolium, blue black (Holly Osmanthus)
Prinsepia sinensis, purple
Prinsepia uniflora, purple-red
Prunus Laurocerasus var. Schipkaensis, black-purple (Cherry-Laurel)
Prunus maritima, purple to crimson (Beach Plum)
Rhodotypos scandens (R. kerrioides) black (White Kerria, Jet-Bead)
Rosa Harisoni, yellow to black (Harison's Yellow Rose)
Sarcococca confusa, black (Sweet Box)
Symplocos paniculata, blue (Sapphire-berry)
Vaccinium angustifolium, blue to black (Lowbush Blueberry)
Vaccinium ovatum, black (Evergreen Blueberry)
Viburnum acerifolium, blue-black (Dockmackie, Maple-leaved Viburnum)
Viburnum cassinoides, black (Withe-rod)
Viburnum dentatum, blue (Arrow-wood)
Viburnum Lentago, blue-black (Sheepberry, Nanny-berry)
Viburnum prunifolium, pink then black (Black-Haw)
Viburnum rhytidophyllum, red finally black (Leather-leaf Viburnum)
Viburnum tinus black (Laurestinus)
Viburnum tomentosum, blue-black (Japanese Snowball)

SHRUBS WITH YELLOW OR ORANGE FRUITS

Cotoneaster Francheti, orange-red

Elaeagnus angustifolia, yellow (Russian Olive)

Euonymus Bungeana, pale yellow to pink

Euonymus Fortunei vegeta, orange-red

Hippophae rhamnoides, orange (Sea-Buckthorn)

Ilex opaca var. Xanthocarpa, yellow (American Holly)

Ligustrum vulgare var. Xanthocarpum, yellow (Common Privet)

Lonicera tatarica var. lutea, yellow (Tatarian Honeysuckle)

Poncirus trifoliata, yellow (Hardy-orange)

Prunus maritima flava, yellow (Beach Plum)

Pyracantha coccinea var. Lalandi, orange-red (Firethorn)

Pyracantha crenulata var. flava, yellow (Firethorn)

Taxus baccata fastigiata var. lutea, yellow (Yew)

Viburnum dilatatum var. xanthocarpum, yellow (Linden Viburnum)

Viburnum Opulus var. xanthocarpum, yellow (European Cranberry-bush)

Viburnum Sargenti var. flavum, yellow

Viburnum setigerum var. aurantiacum, orange-yellow (Tea Viburnum)

Index